What Would You Do?

If This Was Your Last Day On Earth

What they say about the book and the author

"Good advice. Check out Robert's lessons to get yourself to the top of your game. The game of life. "
-**Hoegeng Sjafrudin, Director, BMW-AML Indonesia**

"Robert is a hardworking gentleman with a fascinating life story. We can learn a thing or two from him as we embark on our own journey toward personal success."
- **Paulo Subido, Associate Editor – Top Gear Philippines**

"Experience is perhaps the best educator of life's most important lessons. Robert takes many of his own and condenses them for a unique insight learned over decades of challenges and successes in business, as well as cultivating personal and working relationships with many different people."
-**Vince Pornelos, Editor In Chief, AutoIndustriya.com and C! Magazine**

"Robert's book is a book of courage and transformation with a fresh, pertinent and relevant message for everyone to improve ourselves and challenge us all to live a life with purpose, a positive outlook, and hope as God designed us to be."
- **Atoy Llave, President, Atoy Custom**

"Of the many inspirational books that came out in the market, none of which is best exemplified by a man who have carved his way to the top of his game. Apart from those who have inspired people in words, Robert would inspire you beyond the talk with vision and achievements."
-**Michael Young, President, Japan Home Centre**

"This book is a collection of written words of wisdom and wonder. It is truly an inspiring story."
- **JayR, singer, songwriter, producer**

"This book contains all the elements that you need in order to be inspired, find focus and purpose in life. It has personal stories of the author, peppered with quotes from famous people. I like the chapter on family because truly it's all that matters: Family. You work hard and do everything to achieve your goals in all aspects of your life not just for yourself, but for the people who really matter.

Congratulations Robert for your book! It's a page turner. It's heartfelt and makes the reader think and rethink their priorities & goals in life. It motivates you to become a better person.""
- Christine Babao, Veteran Television Host, Children's Book Author, producer of Moneywise TV

"Robert is a fantastic businessman who keeps a soft, humble heart. His ways are quite confusing to many being a very good businessman and yet generous to everyone. Not a combination seen in many of his peers."
- Ira V. Panganiban, radio broadcaster, Editor Autocar Magazine

"Enjoyed reading and savoring Robert's wisdom. This book is helpful, brilliant and fun."
- Oscar Oida, newscaster, GMA

"I have so much faith in this book and its author. His thirst for knowledge and learning is worth emulating. Age indeed should not be a hindrance to pursue your dreams. And when you have reached your dreams, be like Robert who continues to inspire and help others."
-Delbert Sia, President, D.I.Y. Hardware

"I've known Robert for more than a decade and if I would describe him in one word, it would be PASSIONATE. That's why I'm excited about this book. It reveals his wisdom and his pursuit of excellence in life that we can all learn from".
-Jerome San, CEO, Laurus Enterprise, Official partner of Rich Dad Training S.E.A.

"Robert is passionate about being the best that he can be at what he does. This makes him successful at his job. He is compassionate and shares his blessings and time to other people. He's truly an inspiration to all of us who have been fortunate enough to have worked with him."
- Francine Prieto, actress, host, businesswoman

"Truly inspired by a good person and a great entrepreneur. Robert, may your life story inspire many more people to become entrepreneurs with a true growth mindset.."
- RJ Ledesma, entrepreneur, public speaker, events host

"When I met Robert for the Blade song he was proposing, he brought along his son. There I saw a man who—despite his success—displayed modesty, honesty and love for the company of his family. An admirable guy".
- Jett Pangan, singer, songwriter, performer

"When I met Robert, my first impression of him was that he was just a really positive man with an inspiring story to tell! I am really excited to read about the lessons that he has to share. I'm always ready to learn from great people like Robert!"
-Zahra Bianca Saldua, Ms World Philippines 2013, 2nd Princess

"I had the opportunity to meet Robert in 2016 and I already know he's a successful entrepreneur in the Philippines. This man has a great heart to help other people like him to achieve financial and emotional freedom. Read this book and you will find lots of useful and easy-to-follow steps which would help you achieve the results you truly deserve. At last, a book that gives you a clear roadmap to achieve happiness in your life."
- Jack HM Wong, best-selling author, serial entrepreneur and certified trainer, leader and coach in Blair Singer Training Academy

"Very few books have been written with more heart than this powerful piece. It will surely inspire you to reach for greatness in your life. Great read. Insightful. I could not put it down."
- Melissa Ingkom, nurse practitioner, California, U.S.A.

"That Guy in Red is as passionate about life as the color he is wearing. The first ten minute encounter with him can teach you something about life and that's a privilege I have experienced! More power to you Robert!"
- MJ Marfori, entertainment anchor and correspondent, TV5

"Robert's story is one that is inspiring, that all aspiring entrepreneurs should emulate. So if you want to know more about his life, from building a career within business to putting up his own business, then it is good to read this book."
- Marc Castrodes, motivational speaker, corporate trainer

"From a one peso a month salary to putting up the Philippines' biggest car accessories chain, see the ups and downs, milestones and challenges through the eyes of That Guy In Red behind Blade Auto Center."
- Carl Dy, Property Investment Coach, President, Spectrum

"Robert's book is a testament that if you want something bad enough, it's never too late to get it. This book gives hope to anybody who is still searching for their deeper "why" particularly in the later stages of their lives. Such an inspiring story that allowed me to dream again and move me to my next level."
- Russ Juson, international life coach, transformational leadership facilitator

"I learned a lot from Robert. Despite his achievements, he's really just this warm, friendly and sincere guy who loves to inspire people. Everyone can learn from his life story and apply the same basic principles he talks about in his book to create their own successes in life. If you're just existing and not living, let his book motivate you to move from a life that's ordinary to extraordinary."
- Jenny Ang Dy, GrowingWithJenny.com

"Easy to read, easy to understand and immediately implementable. Great job Robert!"
- Leona Feng, infopreneur, Kuala Lumpur, Malaysia.

"This book offers powerful yet practical tips. True to his mission, Robert's book surely will inspire you to achieve your life goals and shape your own destiny."
- Perrine Jarrault, interior designer, Paris, France.

WHAT WOULD YOU DO?
IF THIS WAS YOUR LAST DAY ON EARTH
First Edition

Published by Blade Asia, Inc.
5/F Blade Auto Center, 108 Timog Avenue, Quezon City, 1103 Philippines

www.ThatGuyInRed.com   **E-mail:** info@ThatGuyInRed.com

First Printing: June 24, 2017
Second Printing: September 17, 2017
Special Edition Paperback ISBN: 978-164008786-6
Amazon.com (Colored) ISBN: 978-621-95716-0-9
Amazon.com (B&W) ISBN: 978-621-95716-1-6
Digital Ebook: 978-621-95716-2-3

ISBN issued by: National Library of the Philippines

What Would You Do?

If This Was Your Last Day On Earth

7 Lessons Life Taught Me

You're <u>NEVER</u> Too Old To Start Over Again!

Robertson Sy Tan

Foreword by Francis Kong

Dedication

To **Mom** and **Dad**
Thank you for teaching and
inspiring me to work hard and
never give up on my dreams.

To **Fanny**
Thank you for your constant support in
all my endeavors and for helping me do
what I love to do.

To my loving wife, **Frances**, who stood by me
when I embarked on my journey to pursue
my passion and career, thank you from the
bottom of my heart. You are inspiringly
compassionate. Together, our strengths
enable us to build the future we hope to
achieve. You are truly my soulmate.

And to God's greatest gifts to my life,
Hannah, **Miles**, **Daryl** and **Redd**, you
are the proof of God's generosity and
the reason I smile. You are the purpose
that drive me to strive for success in
everything.

You are all amazing and I'm truly blessed
to have all of you in my life.

This book is for all of you.

Contents

ACKNOWLEDGEMENT

Thank you!

When I left the corporate world after 20 years of service, I sent out an e-mail to all my colleagues and friends. The e-mail captured all my thoughts during that time and on the subject line, I wrote "Seven Lessons Life Taught Me".

After reading my e-mail, a colleague at work told me that with what I have shared, I should be writing a book.

I never thought that the day would come that I'd see a cover of a book with my name on the byline. The thing is, I made it my mission to share stories and experiences, and to help inspire others to shape their own destinies. This book is one of the tools to accomplish such a mission. It is very close to my heart and is something I'm more than happy to add to my list of things I have done before I turn 50.

As I write this Acknowledgment page, I know that I might leave out hundreds of people who deserve recognition for my progress and success. It's impossible to thank everyone who made an impact in my life and helped me in the development of this book. So if you don't see your name listed below, I apologize to you in advance and I hope you reach out to me so I can thank you personally.

And with that, I'd like to express my infinite thanks and deep appreciation to the many wonderful people who made this book project possible:

Robert Kiyosaki, for sharing your stories which inspired me and helped me change my life direction.

Uncle Neri Tan, for your positive influence and for being a constant inspiration.

Delbert Sia and Winston Lim, for being true friends and encouraging me to keep going.

Sam Liuson and the Wednesday Pitstop Bible Study Group, my prayer warriors, for being true vines, an enduring source of light, joy, learning and unfailing support.

Francis Kong, Jerome San, Gerry Robert, Jackie A. Salipande, Kenneth Chow, Mario Alaman, Debbie Ko Sia, Alexander Uy, Brent Fox, Richard Thomas and Arlo Almorfe for helping me weave my vision into this book which you are holding now.

To all the Bladers, most of whom I can never thank enough. It's an honor working with all of you. Thank you for the commitment, the laughs, the tears, and the transformations I've been privileged enough to witness. Also for cheerfully doing whatever it takes to get the job done.

To my life pegs, for showing me that the most ambitious dreams can come true if you believe they will, and for showing me that with the right amount of passion and determination, good things are bound to happen.

To my 50-year-old self, for giving me the 'Go' signal to aim high and never settle. For not allowing my age to get in the way of accomplishing goals, and to always have the courage to create no matter what.

And most of all, to God, my Savior, who saw me for my potential when I couldn't see it. Thank you, Jesus, for all the challenges that you have introduced in my life—the trials, the people who made things difficult for me, and for all the hurdles I had to overcome. For putting the desire in my heart and helping me to live life to my fullest potential. Thank you for preparing me so I can achieve my higher purpose. ◄▲►

that the most
ambitious dreams
can come true
if you believe
they will

Welcome to the world of the Young

Foreword by Francis Kong

Robert's message is challenging, but is filled with encouragement that empowers the reader to aspire higher, and take life to the next level

*W*hen Robert asked me, "Francis, I have always wanted to write a book; what should I do?" My response to this question has always been the same, "Write!"

I expect nothing less from Robert and wouldn't be surprised if one day I see his book in the memoir or inspirational aisles of my favorite bookstore.

But what I didn't expect to receive was a request from him to write a brief foreword for his book. I was delighted and immediately accepted it because he has a story worth sharing.

Robert's message is challenging, but is filled with encouragement that empowers the reader to aspire higher, and take life to the next level.

Strange, is it not—that certain people would want to achieve something in life and dream to be successful yet have not lifted a finger to make it happen? This is why one pundit said: "In order to make your dreams come true, you need to wake up and do some work."

Work hard. Dream big.
My office at the Blade headquarters.

Robert knows that, like doing business, writing a book needs to have a firm decision to do it now and he does. And in this book he shares life lessons and principles as an entrepreneur, with the hope that those who feel it is hopeless at their current stage of life, would find the courage and the inspiration to do it.

Robert turns 50! That's great. Congratulations for entering into the stage of being young. As you mentioned yourself, age is only a number. Yes it is but it carries a lot of meaning too. And here is what I mean in being 50 and entering the age of being young. Because 49 is the old age of the young and 51 is the young age of the old. ◄▲►

Welcome to the Age
and the World of the Young!

INTRODUCTION

Memento Mori

There is a Latin proverb, memento mori. It means 'remember that you have to die.' I chose to remember it every day of my life, because like everyone knows life is too short. Steve Jobs said, "Death is very likely the single best invention of Life. Remembering that you are going to die is the best way I know to avoid the trap of thinking you have something to lose. You are already naked. There is no reason not to follow your heart."

This is what I remind myself always—not to waste time. When I was introduced to Robert Kiyosaki in 2004, the experience taught me that I need to prepare for my future and it doesn't start with waiting for the right moment, but making every moment right.

When my Uncle Neri died in that same year, this sad event taught me that life is too short to not chase after your dreams. I have to make every day count and today I can be the person who I want to be. It started me on a journey that literally changed my life. I was living every day, one day at a time.

When you know you have no day, no week, or no tomorrow to look forward to, you somehow find a way to leave a part of you to be remembered because *what have you got to lose?* You just push the pedal and live full effort. You let go of inhibitions and cherish everything life has to offer. It is not a license to be careless or reckless, rather it's an opportunity to live more. You choose to be kind. You choose to help one another. You choose to forgive. You choose to do the impossible. And it starts right now!

This is the reason this book exists, and also the reason for its title. If my time is up tomorrow, I have this book to leave behind for my loved ones and share with them things I've learned over time. Now is the time to pass it forward.

How about you? What can you do today that will make you grow and test your limits? Go ahead and live without fear. This is your reminder.

My family. Mom, Dad, Teddy and Andrew.

In The Beginning

I was born into a loving and caring family. I think you can call that lucky or blessed. We grew up in a rented apartment in Baclaran. It cost my parents Php180 or (US $3.50) a month to rent it. Since both my parents were working, we always had food on the table and all my siblings' and my needs were met.

Education is Top Priority

My parents also impressed on us kids that getting an education is the most important legacy they could leave us and they would do anything to support us until we finish schooling. I also remember that it was my mother who took me in to the direction of business. She would always remind me to take a business course—the most practical and low budget course at the time. So, I enrolled in De La Salle University which had a business degree and allowed me to finish the courses as early as possible so I can start my career sooner.

Although we have everything we need, we cannot always have what we want. I remember going out with college friends to fast food joints and I had to order the cheapest item on the menu because I had a meager allowance. I think that's how we were taught the value of money. To get what we want, we had to work hard to earn it.

It was also in college that I met my future wife—Frances. And she knows how creative I was just so I could take her out for dates back then. I knew I had to get a job, so I became a working student at Abenson Appliances.

I was determined to succeed and start off my career right after graduation. Mr. Wilson Lim, Abenson President, took notice of my achievements as top seller and soon after graduating, promoted me to management trainee.

My part-time work enabled me to raise some seed money for a trading business. It also made it possible for Frances and I to wed in 1991. We recently celebrated our 25th wedding anniversary.

Water filters were my first product after graduation.

Focus on Success.
Rewards will naturally follow.

My career was on a roll. I was also offered by an uncle to be the co-founder of a new marketing and distribution company. So, I resigned from my job at Abenson and started this new company with him. I was General Manager and the job was a challenge that I readily accepted even without a solid background or experience in handling a company. I named it Miles&Levels Philippines, inspired by multinational corporations like Proctor&Gamble and Johnson&Johnson. It was named so because I envisioned it to have a wide range of products that when laid down in a straight line, it would run many miles long.

It wasn't easy to get a startup company running. When I was appointed President and CEO by 1991, the company was barely hanging on. To make things worse, my uncle and I weren't on the same page regarding solutions and directions to take for the company. With no clear direction and almost bankrupt, I committed to turn the company around.

This wouldn't be a success story if I didn't succeed. I did succeed and helped it get back on its feet months later. The company was my baby. I dedicated 20 years honing much of my skills in the industry, yet not all good things last.

Team Miles&Levels in Hong Kong Incentive trip for a job very well done.

Enjoy the Good Things while they Last

The reality of it all was I wasn't the owner and no matter how much I invested in this company, it's not my show to run. Somehow I knew my days at the company were almost up because I knew I had to start my own.

In 2004, I was introduced to Robert Kiyosaki, author of Rich Dad, Poor Dad, one of the bestselling self-help books on financial success. I was inspired by Kiyosaki's story about

The best way to predict the future is to create it.

his two dads: the rich successful businessman and the intellectual, but poor dad. I mostly related to poor dad's story, who however good at what he did, always failed because his ideas clash with his boss.

I saw my future in Poor Dad and it was a loud wake up call.

Uncle Neri and Aunt Mercy
In California, 2004

Wrong Place at the Wrong Time

One of my relatives who made an impact in my life was my Uncle Neri, my mentor who helped me widen my contacts and took me along on his sales calls. He was there every step of the way when I was stabilizing Miles&Levels and also one of the reasons I started my business. But one fateful day, he was suddenly taken away from us. His death was a big loss to me and our family.

God showed me the Way

Uncle Neri's death showed me that life is too short. You do not even know if you have tomorrow to live. I knew that God wanted to send me a message and I heard it loud and clear.

Meeting Robert Kiyosaki wasn't a coincidence. His book was meant to put clarity in my path. It showed me the clear steps I needed to take and follow the path of Rich Dad and do everything I needed to do to forge a better future for my family. Being employed won't make me sustainable; I need to generate.

Uncle Neri's death is the basis of my present day core value that life is too short. What can I do today to make my life more meaningful? He taught me the ropes of the business and got me connected with some of his top clients. His untimely death pushed me to take immediate action. It all tied up well in the end.

I met Kiyosaki and I had to hear his story because I knew I had to fire my boss and start my own business. My uncle's death showed me that I have to start living now. If I am to start my own business, I shouldn't hesitate because there may be no tomorrow.

What Would You Do?

If This Was Your Last Day On Earth

These 12 words became very clear in my mind. These were the words that set everything in motion for me to start my own company. If today were your last day, have you done everything you've planned? Would you still hold that grudge or would you forgive those who have wronged you? Would those offenses still matter when you have no tomorrow? I made the decision. Although it came later in my career, it was the moment my life began.

Life begins at 40

I was 37 when I made the life-changing decision to start my own company. But age is just a number. I wasn't young yet it was like my life was slowly unfolding . It was just then that I was starting to live every day. It began when I decided to take charge and put up my own business. Starting all over must be well-thought out. I came up with a five-year cycle of starting up a business, and if I have only one or two of these five-year cycles, then I must hurry up.

But the main excitement of my life came when I had a chance meeting with SM Malls' Harley Sy at one of my kids' swimming party. We talked about ideas and I pitched to him the car accessories retail store idea. Sy told me that it is a niche unfilled and a good direction to take.

With that, Blade's journey began.

Francine Prieto, Jinno Rufino and the Hotwire Group.

If you Build it, They will Come.

As soon as I made the declaration, ideas started to pour in—store images, designs, and merchandise all came to us easily. My competitors became my allies. We were on our way to what will be known today as the country's top automotive accessories retail chain— Blade Auto Center.

Success occurs when your dreams get bigger than your excuses.
Department of Trade and Industry (DTI) and Philippine Retailer
Association
2006 Outstanding Retailer Awards Night.

Rejections are Blessings in Disguise.

Like any other startup, I experienced a lot of road blocks along the way. First, we were not so lucky to get a space at Karport, Fort Bonifacio, so I had to start looking elsewhere. But as they say, when a door closes, another one opens.

The Ayala Group was set to build a mall near Karport. Of course malls have lots of parking slots. And that would mean more cars and that would mean a large percentage of shoppers own cars—our target customers.

Blade Auto Center was a fresh concept and we were immediately accepted as one of the tenants.

What's in a Name?

People often ask me, 'Why did you name your company Blade?' My quickest answers are, 'It's a simple, short name that is easy to recall,' or 'It is edgy, and is quite catchy.'

But, there is another reason behind the name.

A while back, when we were in the beginning stages, we had almost zero experience in retail. We had very little start-up capital and we were about to embark in an unfamiliar territory.

We pored through history books and found our man: Andres Bonifacio. He and his valiant organization the *Kataastaasang, Kagalanggalangan na Katipunan ng mga Anak ng Bayan* became our inspiration. Bonifacio fought for the country's freedom and independence from the Spanish rule. It was an uphill battle. He and his team were up against heavily armed soldiers with guns and cannons. Yet with sheer determination, armed with just their swords or *bolo*, they were able to rise to victory.

We were told that in retail, names are critical. It should be remembered (quick recall). When customers see it, it should register and stick immediately. It should be easy to pronounce and spell and connect to customers. Andres Bonifacio's weapon stuck with us. The *bolo* or sword became the symbol of the challenge we were about to take. The sword's cutting edge symbolizes how we want to be known—a cutting edge business that is fresh, innovative, and energetic. We made the name trendier. The sword has a sharp edge, hence we called ourselves **BLADE**.

When there's an open door, people stop by.
Blade Auto Center at a major shopping mall.

One Plus One Equals 13

Armed with the attitude and mindset of living like there was no tomorrow, the company started accepting mall offers to lease spaces. Since the economy was bad and retail stores were not expanding, mall operators were offering good prime spaces for serious takers. We were dead serious.

In order to establish a retail business, we needed to set up a store network. The brand was needed to be noticed by suppliers as well as customers and the only way to achieve that is by being everywhere.

The first Blade Auto Center opened at Market! Market!, BGC. September 17, 2004

Three months after the company opened the first store, we opened a second branch which was then Park Square Makati. Then a third store at SM Southmall and the fourth at Robinsons Manila soon followed. A total of six stores were opened in our first year and another seven were operational by the following year for a total of 13 stores in two years. The brand became an instant market leader, a chain store that suppliers could not ignore.

We kept the momentum going year after year. As of this writing, Blade operates 50 locations nationwide.

That Guy In Red.
Thanksgiving Day with the Blade family.

I live every day as though there is no tomorrow. Since that fateful day of my favorite uncle's passing, I realized that life is too short. And the thought that death can come for any of us at any moment at any given time. My wife and I decided to live in the moment.

Before leaving for work, Frances and I would exchange favors beginning with the phrase, "If I am not around tomorrow, please do this for me..." It has become our way of saying, 'I love you.' We were so ready to the point that we even have our own memorial lot and service ready, just in case. I even told her that during my funeral, I want to break traditions and request that everyone wear red, which is taboo in the Chinese culture.

And so, by making those little steps, we erase any anxieties about the future and instead learning to embrace the 'Now,' we dared to go after our dreams one by one.

Blade was founded on this 12—word philosophy. My life is blessed today because God helped me change my life and shaped my destiny through these words. ➊➊

Life begins at 40

Be proud of your age because with age comes wisdom. Every day is a new opportunity to learn and we should not waste it on unproductive behavior or attitudes.

1

"The belief that life begins at is a myth

4

*R*esearch has found that the fourth decade heralds the beginning of the end. A study of 2,282 people aged 18 to 87 found that hitting 40 was synonymous with forgetfulness, lack of concentration, and poor focus. While general intelligence appeared to remain stable over time, psychologists concluded that everyday mental skills, such as remembering a telephone number or a person's name, showed a marked decline from the age of 40 onwards.[1]

Can you imagine if I actually read and believed this piece of information during my late 30s? I don't think I would have had the courage to pursue and run my own business.

Although it is a fact that with age comes the decline of all the mental faculties and physical capacity of the human body, I believe it's the power of the mind that can make us reach our full potential, whatever our age is or stage we are at in life.

---

[1] Nicole Martin. "Life Begins At Forty - and Don't You Forget It". Telegraph.Co.Uk, December ,2000. http://www.telegraph.co.uk/news/health/1378861/Life-begins-at-forty-and-dont-you-forget-it.html. (accessed Apr.12,2017)

0

Legally Drive — **17**

18 — **Legally Adult**

Legally Drink — **21**

} Realize You're Getting Old

Old — **40**

One example of a man who met success later on his life is fried chicken mogul, Colonel Harland Sanders. Sanders' motel and restaurant business began to dwindle, but it was also around that time that he perfected his recipe and technique for cooking the now world-famous 'finger-lickin' good' fried chicken, which he peddled door to door to houses and restaurants for four cents. He was aged 65.

During the Renaissance, life expectancy was 25 years old. With limited medical expertise and plagues ravaging continents, illness often was a death sentence. Reaching 40 was a feat. By the 1930s, however, things started to change. The new century brought advances in health and medicine- illnesses like tuberculosis, pneumonia, or small pox, no longer were death sentences. People were able to enjoy their senior years with good health. Families began to extend and great grandparents were able to see the birth of their great-grandchildren.

As wine gets better with age, so does the human capacity, it seems so too for a lot of things. For me, age is just a number. It shouldn't limit one's capacity to aim for better things in life just because society dictates that your age means you're nearing the end of your career.

I was 37 when Frances and I made the decision to put up our own business. At that time and stage in my life, there's really not much room for mistakes. I was at a point when I was not that young to be full of energy, yet at the same time not that old to be passive and laid back.

● ● ●

PITSTOP ⬤

"A person is made to be something. One must only learn to recognize that potential to realize that."

—Robertson Sy Tan, ThatGuyInRed.com

Dream big. What should I do next?
Reflected on it during a visit to
the White House at Ronald Reagan Library.

I realized that it's never too late to become who I'm meant to be. Often quoted, it must ring true, "A person is made to be something. One must only learn to recognize that potential to realize that."

Anxiety overtook me, but I welcomed it. I knew then something had to change.

YEAR 1

Conception or establishment of the business

YEAR 2

Introduction of the business and products

YEAR 3

Gaining customers or not

YEAR 5

Expansion or Shut Down

YEAR 4

Continued growth or problem stabilizing

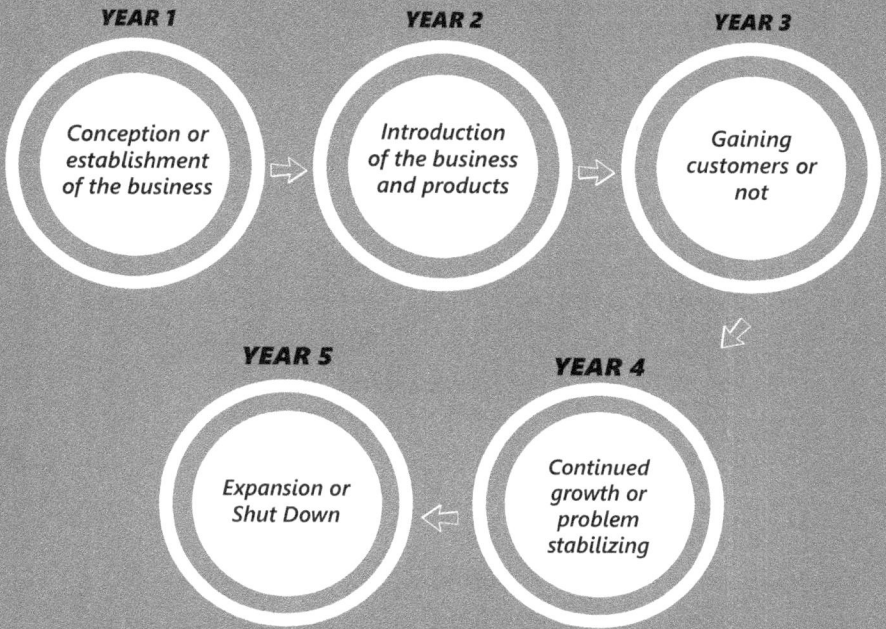

Knowing this (and I bet I wouldn't have known this if I was 15 years younger) I thought to myself, How many more five-year cycles do I have? At my age, I thought I only had one or two left. And it's enough to go through with it and risk it. I really have to make it this time. Failure is never an option.

● ● ●

PITSTOP ●

The knowledge that you have emerged wiser and stronger from setbacks means that you are, ever after, secure in your ability to survive. You will never truly know yourself, or the strength of your relationships, until both have been tested by adversity. Such knowledge is a true gift, for all that it is painfully won, and it has been worth more than any qualification I ever earned.

**—J.K. Rowling,
British novelist and author of
best-selling books the *Harry Potter* series**

When I say life begins at 40, I don't mean that you have to be 40 to start or pursue your dreams. For me, it doesn't matter what age or stage you are in life to pursue your dream, it just started for me that way. I put my dream on the back burner, because I was too busy chasing the corporate dream. But nearing my 40's, I was wiser and more decisive. Yes, I'm making wise decisions and that is the crux of the matter.

At 40, I had the maturity to enlarge my life and outlook. I gained knowledge and wisdom through hard times.

The salesmen. Top sales executive team with Nonong Lojo (second from the left) and Ernie Angeles in 1994.

When I was young, I was insecure and fearful of judgment. Twenty something is that age when you are hungry for the acceptance of your peers. You may be more daring and susceptible to making mistakes. And I believe that after making those mistakes and being judged, fear no longer has a grasp on you. It's a clean slate. You know how it feels. You survived it and you know the pitfalls to avoid; experience serves you well.

For most of us, life happens and all our dreams just get sidetracked. But there will always be that instance that 'big dream' will be calling out your name. I knew I had to act upon it.

I know the feeling of being burned out at work. Although I was already in a good position in my career then, there was this feeling that would pound on my chest. I knew that I had to pursue my passion. It scared me. But it felt good to be scared, because I knew I'm alive and I need to do something about it. It's what's keeping me up all night and it means it's important.

PITSTOP ⬤

Your work is going to fill a large part of your life, and the only way to be truly satisfied is to do what you believe is great work. And the only way to great work is to love what you do.

—Steve Jobs, Apple CEO

The Red Event 1997

Work is love made visible, according to author and humanitarian Kahlil Gibran. And it's true, you cannot have the passion for something and not love what you do. And the only way you can put in as much effort and work into something is when you truly love what you're doing.

Whoever said that work cannot be fun? I really loved what I was doing. Time flew fast as we achieved our company goals one after the other. I was very happy with my team and my work despite having difficulty adjusting to my boss. For me, that was a good indicator that I wasn't working to my full potential and I needed to shift.

It was during that time that I was already contemplating to pursue my big dreams. I've even crafted out the 'big lessons' in my life that have proven to be transformative. Soon after, I made the commitment to follow my dream.

PITSTOP

So many of us choose our path out of fear disguised as practicality...You can fail at what you don't want. So you might as well take a chance on doing what you love.

—Jim Carrey, graduation speech at Maharishi University of Management

Ralph Waldo Emerson once said, "Nothing great has ever been achieved without enthusiasm."

Economics professor Larry Smith of the University of Waterloo, TEDx (Technology, Entertainment, Design) delivers a lecture on career success titled, "Why You Will Fail to Have a

the motivation I had was my family, that's why I needed to succeed in this endeavor

Great Career." In his lecture, Smith talks about 'plenty of bad jobs, high-stress, blood-sucking, soul-destroying jobs. Then there are great jobs, but very little in between." Smith says most people will fail to land a great job or enjoy a great career because they are afraid to follow their passion. Find and use your passion and you'll have a great career. Don't do it and you won't. [2]

When you're nearing your 40's, there is no coasting. There's only up or down

Attitude is everything. You're not 25 and there'll be little room for mistakes. If you want to start over, you need to stick to your guns. You need to be sure of your steps. The motivation I had was my family, that's why I needed to succeed in this endeavor.

The phrase "life begins at 40" was coined by Walter Pitkin who wrote the book of the same title. It was a self-help book he wrote in 1932. In the book, he said at 40, one can still look forward to many years of usefulness and fun if you keep a positive attitude. [3]

Your youth may be over, but there are as many opportunities in this day and age to live more meaningful lives. But if you're sitting in a corner and thinking that life is about to end, then life will give up on you as well. At 37, instead of panicking and moping that my career was about to end, I instead took it as the beginning of a new phase in my life.

I was more confident and more determined than I was when younger.

---

[2] Carmine Gallo. *Talk Like TED*. 1st ed. (London: Macmillan, 2014), p24.

[3] "Life Begins At 40?!". *Life Starts At*.http://www.lifestartsat.com/life-begins-40/. (accessed Apr 12, 2017)

PITSTOP ⬤

Two seeds lay side by side in the fertile soil. The first seed said, "I want to grow! I want to send my roots deep into the soil beneath me, and thrust my sprouts through the earth's crust above me ... I want to unfurl my tender buds like banners to announce the arrival of spring ... I want to feel the warmth of the sun on my face and the blessing of the morning dew on my petals!"

And so she grew...

The second seed said, "Hmmmm. If I send my roots into the ground below, I don't know what I will encounter in the dark. If I push my way through the hard soil above me I may damage my delicate sprouts ... what if I let my buds open and a snail tries to eat them? And if I were to open my blossoms, a small child may pull me from the ground. No, it is much better for me to wait until it is safe."

And so she waited...

A yard hen scratching around in the early spring ground for food found the waiting seed and promptly ate it. [4]

[4] Jack Canfield et al. *Chicken Soup for the Soul* 20th Anniversary Ed (Connecticut: Chicken Soup for the Soul Publishing, LLC, 2013), http://www.chickensoup.com/book-story/36244/risking. (accessed January 2017)

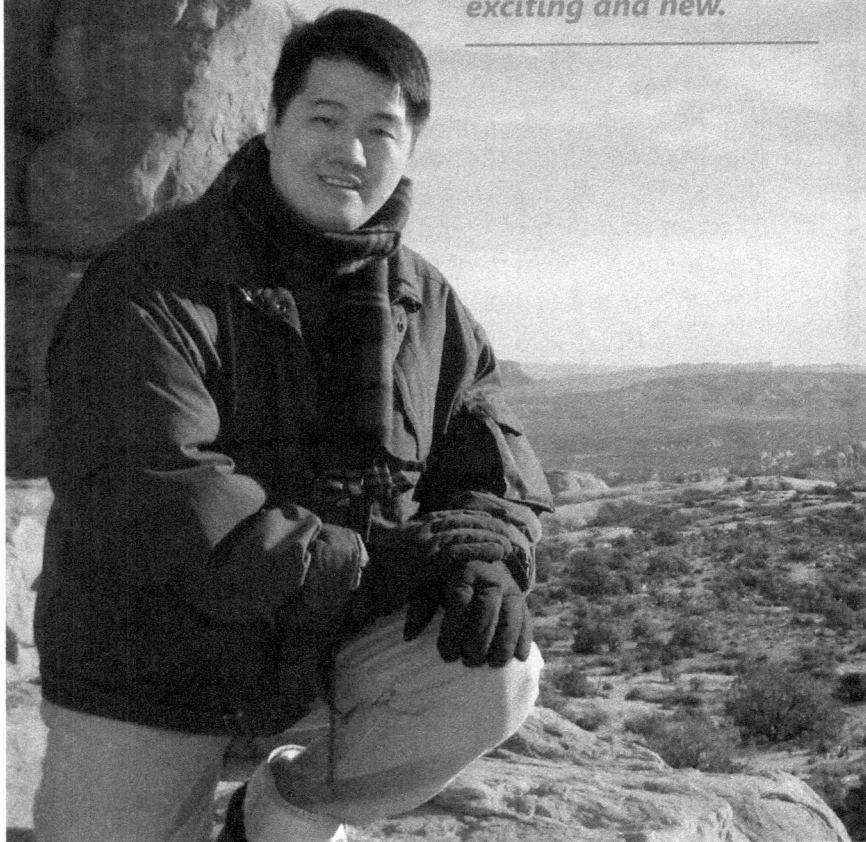

Age is not just about numbers, it's about attitude. One can be 40 and find life still exciting and new.

Some '20 Somethings' felt that life has given up on them. For me, I found the courage to go ahead and green light my dream. Work is going to fill a large part of my life, and the only way I knew I can truly feel satisfied is if I find work that I truly love and believe in. It's about not settling for the next best thing.

It can be daunting to start over. There will be times when you will be doubting yourself, but don't let that doubt overcome you. Just know that you're feeling it, but never let your emotion get the best of you. Emotions are fleeting. I focus on goals and how to follow through each plan.

Just like in sports. Athletes always say that sports are 90% mental and 10% physical performance. This is what differentiates elite athletes from mediocre ones. An athlete can only do so much to train and take care of their bodies, but it's all in the mindset.

Dr. Kirsten Race, Ph.D., brain-based mindfulness solutions expert says, "When our brains get caught up in thoughts from the past...or thoughts of the future...it creates a stress response." This mental chatter can make it difficult to maintain perspective and focus.

Thoughts, emotions, and internal dialogue also affects our behavior. "What we're telling ourselves affects what we see, and what we see affects what we feel" says mental conditioning coach Trevor Moawad. Recent studies by researchers at Coventry University and Staffordshire University found that increased stress and anxiety, including fear of failure, does affect athletic performance in competitive situations.[5]

As I neared the age of 40, I knew that I had to change my mindset that it is the end of my career. I, instead, cultivated a growth mindset. I didn't believe what society says that careers will be over by 40. I believed that I'm in control of my destiny and I can fulfill my dreams.

---

[5] Christine Yu, "Mindfulness For Athletes: The Secret To Better Performance?". *Life By Daily Burn*, June 10, 2014, http://dailyburn.com/life/fitness/mindfulness-techniques-athletes/. (accessed Apr.12,2017)

PITSTOP

There once was a speedy hare who bragged about how fast he could run. Tired of hearing him boast, Slow and Steady, the tortoise, challenged him to a race. All the animals in the forest gathered to watch.

Hare ran down the road for a while and then paused to rest. He looked back at Slow and Steady and cried out, "How do you expect to win this race when you are walking along at your slow, slow pace?"

Hare stretched himself out alongside the road and fell asleep, thinking, "There is plenty of time to relax."

Slow and Steady walked and walked. He never, ever stopped until he came to the finish line.

The animals who were watching cheered so loudly for Tortoise, they woke up Hare.
Hare stretched and yawned and began to run again, but it was too late. Tortoise was over the line.

After that, Hare always reminded himself, "Don't brag about your lightning pace, for Slow and Steady won the race!" [6]

[6] Story Arts Online. *"The Tortoise And The Hare"*. Storyarts.Org.
https://www.storyarts.org/library/aesops/stories/tortoise.html. (accessed Apr.12,2017)

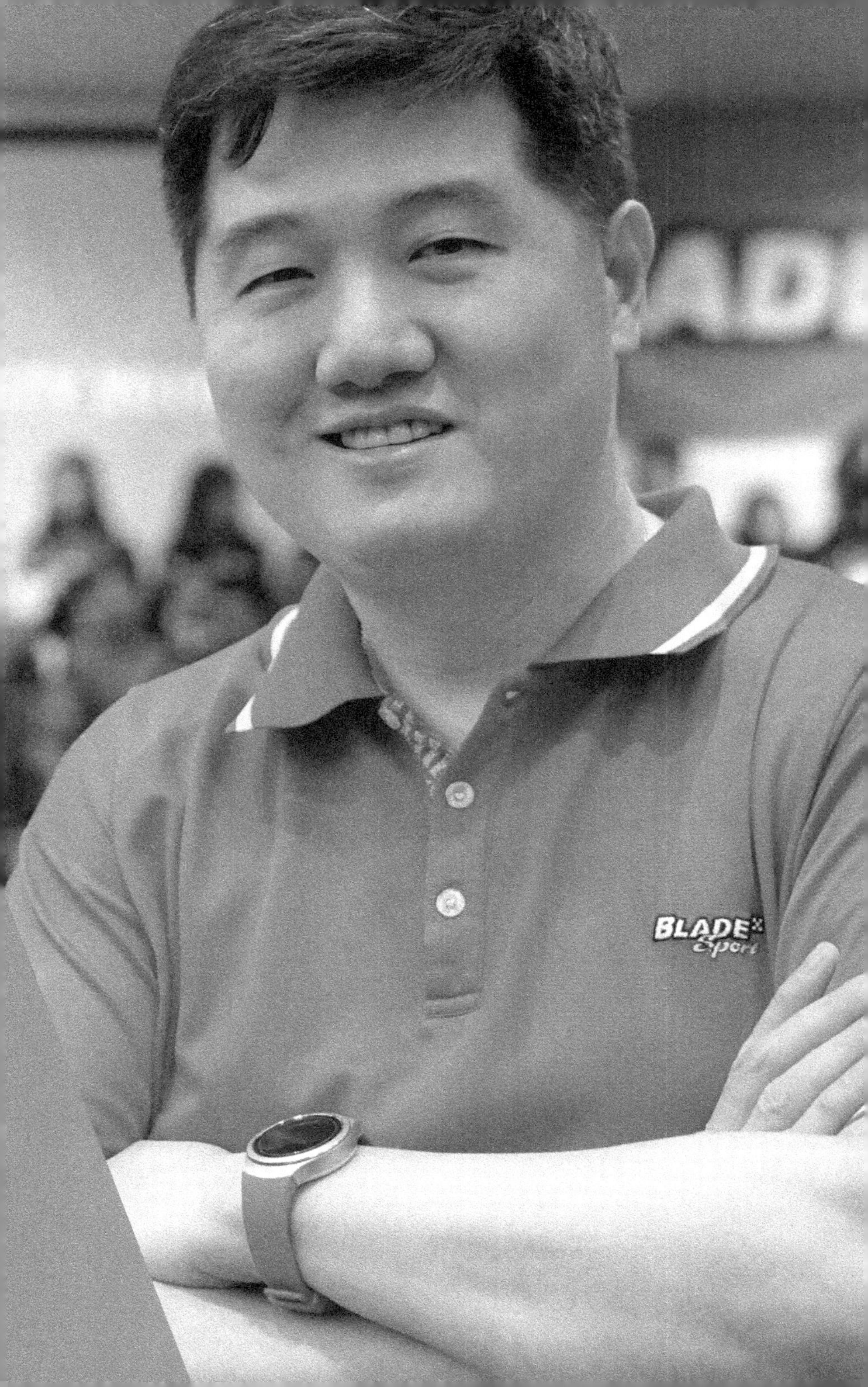
BLADE
Sport

You'll have to be ODD to be number ONE.

> *Having the courage to stick to your goal*
> *is what will set you up for greater things.*
> **—Robertson Sy Tan,**
> **ThatGuyInRed.com**

Remember the fable about the Tortoise and the Hare?

Certain he would win the race, the hare became complacent and went to sleep during the race. I mean a hare vs a tortoise!? All bets are on the hare to win, right? But the tortoise believed that if he worked hard, he had as much chance of winning. And he did!

There are two mindsets at play. The hare had a **fixed mindset**. The hare knows that he would win the race because of his ability. Based from his experience, he always wins.

The tortoise, on the other hand, had a **growth mindset**. He knows well that he is slow compared to the hare. But he also knows that hard work can also help him win. He's not afraid of failure or he would never have agreed to race the hare.

The tortoise has the ability to press on. That ability to persevere and never give up is what I believe makes all the difference. I knew then that I must never give up on my dream.

One has to have grit. Grit, which according to Merriam-Webster is the 'firmness of character; indomitable spirit,' is an important element in success. According to American psychologist and author Angela Lee Duckworth it is the 'passion and perseverance to stick to long-term goals'. It is the quality of 'sticktoitiveness' to a goal which enables someone to reach their goal. And I believe at 40, we all have learned that patience is a virtue. Slow and steady wins the race. Having the courage to stick to your goal, your plan no matter what it is, is what will set you up for greater things. And at 40, I think one has more focus at the task at hand.

I'm now 50 years old, and my life is a lot different than it was 13 years ago. If I'd listen to the naysayers, I wouldn't be writing this book and sharing what I've learned. I'm a living, breathing proof that it's possible to be successful even at a later stage in life.

Another famous person of our time, John Lennon, wrote a song titled Life Begins at 40. He wrote it in 1980, the year he turned 40. ◆▲▶

JUMPSTART

- It's never too late to start on a new project or pursue a life-long dream. It's all about the attitude.

- You need to love and commit to something to actually achieve your dreams.

- You're not getting younger; don't let setbacks hold you back. Cultivate a growth mindset, the mindset that there's room for improvement through hard work.

- If you plan on pursuing that dream, you should have grit or the ability to stick to long-term goals.

It's a long road but it's worth it.

Never forget who was with you from the Start

Friends may come and go. Jobs or businesses can be changed. Money can be earned. But our family will always be there. We are born with a set of family members and the policy is "no return, no exchange".

That is why no matter how good, or sometimes not so good, you may think they are, we should always find a way to value the relationship above anything else. Painful as it may be in some cases, be ready to make personal sacrifices for the sake of keeping the relationship. It's the only one you've got.

00.00

Lesson

2

*Fidel and Nelly Tan,
my parents*

When I talk about my family, I always talk from experience. Everyone belongs to a family, whatever kind it is, the biological or adopted one, everyone must have come from somewhere, where one first learned their values and principles in life.

According to the World Family Organization, the family is the basic unit of society. It is central for the transmission of human values and the development of individuals into responsible and self-reliant personalities.[7]

The family is the nucleus of civilization and the basic social unit of society. Aristotle wrote that the family is nature's established association for the supply of mankind's everyday wants.[8]

I consider myself extremely lucky. I was born into a loving and caring family. In this day and age, being born to a family with parents together, working hard to take care of their kids is a true blessing. Although my parents did not have to struggle to put food on the table, we were also not rich enough to get whatever we wanted while growing up.

---

[7] "World Family Organization brochure. www.worldfamilyorganization.org/brochure.pdf. (accessed January 2017)

[8] William Bennett, "Stronger Families, Stonger Societies," *The New York Times*, http://www.nytimes.com/roomfordebate. (accessed January 2017)

My family

Like many young married couples, my parents started out renting an apartment in Baclaran for Php180.00 (USD $3.50) a month. It was our first home. It provided shelter, not only for us, but also for my aunts who were also starting their own careers.

As a child raised by working parents, I was taught to value education. My parents instilled in us that education is the most important asset or 'pamana' that they could leave us. It is priceless. It is a treasure that no one can ever steal from us nor can it be lost; hence we should value it.

Like any other kid with Chinese heritage, my parents also instilled in us the value of self-discipline. I can say my upbringing also highlighted the importance of hard work and that which I can attribute to my success.

Looking ahead into the future.
Me at Chiang Kai Shek College, Grade School, 1974

My parents were generous. They were committed to provide for our education, but when it comes to luxuries, my siblings and I were taught early on to work for it. One experience that taught me that success won't be handed to you, instead you should strive for it was a trip to a fast-food restaurant.

I distinctly remember when McDonald's entered the local food industry. It was a game changer at the time. Everyone wanted a taste of their burgers. It was the "it" place to be in and be seen back in the day. I remember that time, when my 'barkada'—some with girlfriends in tow—and I went to McDonald's for the first time right after semester break.

Everyone ordered those big burgers, fries, with drinks, even treating their girlfriends to those meals. Except me. I ordered the most basic burger since I had a meager allowance and little extra money. It was an experience I'd never forget for my entire life. I had what every millennial would say a FOMO (fear of missing out) moment, and I never wanted to feel that way again. So from that day on, I vowed to myself that I want to be successful so I can have enough money in my pocket to enjoy life's comforts.

Chiang Kai Shek College, High School Batch 84, Highschool Barkada at the 30th Anniversary Reunion

PITSTOP ⬤

*It's not how good you are,
it's how good you want to be.*

**—Paul Arden, It's Not How Good You Are,
It's How Good You Want to Be**

My Mom, although she's not a Tiger mom (a type of restrictive parenting ascribed to Asians according to author Amy Chua's memoir *The Battle Hymn of the Tiger Mom*), would always remind me to take up a business course in college. Aside from being the most affordable course at the time, it was the most practical and most useful subject. I guess she knew from the start that I would be engaging myself in business somewhere down the line.

I entered college with the mindset of starting a career early. I chose De La Salle University because it operates under the trimestral system. This means instead of having two semesters in a school year, the university would have three. This, I thought to myself, would mean I'd graduate earlier than most of my batch mates from high school. This also meant that I can start early with my career.

Since I did not have extra allowance for anything other than my schooling, I worked at Abenson Appliances during school breaks. I was among the top sales persons for calculators, television sets, cassette recorders, and musical instruments. Sometimes I would intentionally put a wide time gap when I enroll to allow me to walk to Harrison Plaza to work. Money I earned as a working student was then used as a seed for a very small trading business and to date my girlfriend.

We are young.
With my soul mate, Frances.

Shortly after graduating from college, Abenson President, Mr. Wilson Lim promoted me as management trainee. He wanted me to head the office automation department of the retail chain. It was also around that time that another uncle offered me to be the co-founder of a new marketing and distribution company.

Miles & Levels Philippines Opened its doors on March 1, 1988

We introduced household water filters in 1988

The offer intrigued me. Being able to build something from scratch has always been attractive to me so I resigned from Abenson and started this new company. My uncle is the head of a very successful manufacturing company focused on selling construction products. This new company is supposed to focus on household products untapped by the parent business. It was a real challenge—an exciting one at that.

Family. Where life begins and love never ends

Drawing inspiration from multinational corporations like Proctor&Gamble and Johnson&Johnson, I named the company Miles&Levels Philippines. It was named such because I envisioned this company to have a wide range of products, that if you were to lay them in a straight line on the ground, it would run many miles long. Its range would cater to various levels in the market. I wanted this company to be just as big as other foreign companies.

To say that starting up was a steep uphill battle is an understatement. Back then, I had no experience. Being a start-up, the company had no clear directions and was in a constant struggle to make enough for the rent and overhead. To compound the situation, my uncle and I could not agree on the solutions and directions to take for the company. It was also the start of a rift between my uncle and I.

The rift caused all sorts of problems that trickled down to other family members. It was one of the challenges I had to face. It was disheartening, yet I could not let it affect my relationship with him as my uncle.

PITSTOP ⬤

The Bridge

Once upon a time two brothers who lived on adjoining farms fell into conflict. It was the first serious rift in 40 years of farming side by side. They had been sharing machinery, trading labor and goods as needed without a hitch. Then the long collaboration fell apart. It began with a small misunderstanding and it grew into a major difference which exploded into an exchange of bitter words followed by weeks of silence.

One morning there was a knock on elder brother's door. He opened it to find a man with a carpenter's toolbox. "I am looking for a few days of work", he said. "Perhaps you would have a few small jobs here and there. Could I help you?"

"Yes!" said the elder brother. "I do have a job for you. Look across the creek at that farm. That's my neighbor, in fact, it's my younger brother and we don't get along. Last week he dug a wider passage for water into his farm. But he ended up creating a very wide creek in between our farms and I am sure he did it just to annoy me. I want you to build me something so that we don't have to stand and see each other's face from across."

The carpenter said "I think I understand the situation. I will be able to do a job that will please you." The elder brother had to go to town for supplies, so he helped the carpenter get the materials ready and then he was off for the day. The carpenter worked hard all that day measuring, sawing, nailing.

At sunset when the elder brother returned, the carpenter had just finished his job. The elder brother's eyes opened wide and his jaw dropped. It was not what he had even thought of or imagined. It was a bridge stretching from one side of the creek to the other! A fine piece of work, beautiful handrails. And to his surprise, his younger brother across the creek was coming to meet him with a big smile and arms wide open to hug him.

"You are really kind and humble my brother! After all I had done and said to you, you still shown that blood relations can never be broken! I am truly sorry for my behaviour", the younger brother said as he hugged his elder brother. They turned to see the carpenter hoist his toolbox on his shoulder. "No, wait! Stay a few days. I have a lot of other projects for you," said the older brother.

"I'd love to stay on", the carpenter said, "but, I have many more bridges to build!"

Moral: There is no shame in accepting your mistake or forgiving each other. We should be kind and humble. We should try to stay together as a family and not break away from it over the petty arguments.[9]

---

[9] The Bridge." MoralStories.org. http://www.moralstories.org/the-bridge/ (accessed January 2017)

Leo Tolstoy once wrote "All happy families are alike: each unhappy family is unhappy in its own way". Being part of a clan or tribe promotes a feeling of acceptance, like-mindedness, protection, and respect. Studies also have shown that close family ties promote happiness and eventually raise successful individuals, there are, however, a few inimitable individuals who rise in spite of negative kin.

But family is family. Whether we like it or not it's better to keep the peace, especially if good outweighs bad. It is worth trying to stay put and build up. Family life can be the best of times. Bolstering family life is a great investment because meaningful connections lead to success. If those bonds are biological, it is convenient and comforting.[10]

Your family will not only be your best allies, but they can also be your worst critics. Maybe because they know you so well that they can pinpoint your weaknesses. Yet instead of taking a stab at them, learn to understand and listen. Understand where they are coming from. Don't let emotions get the best of you; nothing can hurt you if you won't let them.

In a big family, there will always be misunderstandings and unmet expectations of everybody else. There will always be favorites and there will always be someone least liked, but no matter how difficult a family member may be or how rude or how insensitive, family is family. You can not break away, therefore, you should rebuild the relationship, because in the end, these difficult persons in your life will serve as those cuts which mold you to be the diamond that you are.

● ● ●

---

[10] Carrie Brown, M.D., "Happy Families Are Not All Alike,"*Psychology Today*, http://wwwpsychologytoday.com/blog/the-creativity-cure (Oct.17,2014)

PITSTOP ⬤

*Rejoice with your family in the
beautiful land of life.*

—Albert Einstein

Family shouldn't be treated as an afterthought, but a priority. Work and jobs can be replaced anytime, but a family is irreplaceable. Don't let time pass by without knowing your kids or your spouse. Spend time to bond with your parents.

Strive to find a work-life balance. Having a job should not mean giving up your favorite activities or down-time with people who need you. The work place can only do so much for you, but it shouldn't take the place of family. No matter if you lose or you fail, your family will be your number one support system. Besides, monetary gain is nothing if you have nothing to inspire you to work hard or you don't have a greater purpose. Family provides that purpose. It's the reason why you

This is us.
Clockwise: Hannah, Redd,
Frances, Daryl, Miles and me.

work hard. It's the reason why you want to be successful. I know it's my reason. I want a secured life for my wife and kids, and this is what drove me to put up my own company.

If you want to succeed, disconnect from work and spend time with family. Not only do you find time to relax and recharge but you find inspiration for work. Making time for things that are important to you allows you to find a different perspective, and maybe find a solution to a work-related problem.

> **PITSTOP** ⬤
>
> *My favorite things in life don't cost any money. It's really clear that the most precious resource we all have is time.*
>
> **—Steve Jobs, Apple founder and CEO**

The most successful people know how to use their time wisely. They don't spend it on entertainment, instead they spend their time trying to improve themselves and catching up with family and friends. They work extra hard, but they value their free time. You see, money does not bring us joy, but our relationships do. Don't let a crisis tell you to put your family first in order to spend time with them. Don't let success be attached with regrets as missing out on your daughter's first ballet recital or your son's basketball game. They only get to be kids once.

Put time into what's important. These relationships will be essential to your success because family and loved ones will be the ones pulling you through and celebrating your success. ◄►

Family is not just an important thing.
It is EVERYTHING.

JUMPSTART

- Everyone is born into a family from which an individual learns about himself, his values, and principles in life.

- Family members are your best allies and also your worst critics. Don't sacrifice relationships just because of misunderstandings. Empathize and rebuild the relationship.

- Put time into what's important. In the end, your family will be the ones who will celebrate with you in your success.

Choose the Right Heroes

Your actions are often manifested by your thoughts. That is why you need to choose the right hero to serve as your inspiration. Review your goals. Choose a role model who has achieved success and follow his or her path towards success. Think and do as what your heroes would. Just be sure and clear that it is the future you want.

Lesson

3

*I*ndian civil rights leader Mahatma Gandhi once said, "Keep your thoughts positive because your thoughts become your words. Keep your words positive, because your words become your behavior. Keep your behavior positive, because your behavior becomes your habits. Keep your habits positive, because your habits become your values. Keep your values positive, because your values become your destiny."

If you're a Star Wars fan, it's similar to Master Yoda's famous line, "Fear leads to anger. Anger leads to hate. Hate leads to suffering." Of course, this line is the opposite of being positive. It cultivates a negative thought which is fear, which leads to a negative reaction and in turn results to a negative outcome.

Your daily thoughts can be assimilated in every aspect of our lives. We must be careful of our thoughts, because what we think often comes out of our mouth which can be heard by people around us. Thoughts, when spoken, can create change. If you observe a calm lake and you throw rocks at it, the rocks create ripples in the water. Just like that, words create ripples. These words leave a mark. It can make an impact in our lives, and in the lives of people around us.

Words when spoken can affect behavior. Words can inspire, motivate, but also break. Behavior becomes a part of our character. Our personality is molded by how we behave in various situations, so our behavior affects our actions.

An action done repetitively becomes a habit. That's why if you want to make reading a book a habit, you have to repeat this action every day. Studies show that all it takes is 21 days to form a new habit. So if you want to cultivate a good habit and stick to it, you need to do something regularly making it a part of your daily routine. If you want to change your eating habits to a healthier one, you need to be diligent about your food choices and eat a healthy meal every day. And as these habits become part of your life, these result to a better, healthier you in the future.

Hence, your thought process can influence your path in life. Something you do repetitively will eventually result in who you will become. I believe so and I know so, because I did so.

"Thoughts when spoken can create change."

Be thankful for your hard times,
for they have made you.

PITSTOP

We are what we repeatedly do.
Excellence then, is not an act, but a habit.

—Aristotle

As I've discussed earlier, the mind is a powerful thing. Exceptional athletes, child prodigies, great leaders—all have harnessed their brains to function in a way which ordinary people haven't. Your thoughts are a catalyst for self-perpetuating cycles. What you think directly influences how you feel and how you behave. So if you think you're a failure, you'll feel like a failure. Then, you'll act like a failure, which reinforces your belief that you must be a failure.

Creating a more positive outlook, however, can lead to better outcomes. Optimistic thoughts lead to productive behavior, which increases your chances of a successful outcome.[11]

In 2004, I was introduced to Robert Kiyosaki. He's the author of one of the bestselling financial books of all time *Rich Dad Poor Dad*.

---

[11] Amy Morin, "This Is How Your Thoughts Become Your Reality," *Forbes*, http://www.forbes.com/sites/amymorin/2016/06/15/this-is-how-your-thoughts-become-your-reality/#6f9d042d6e03. (accessed February 28, 2017)

I saw my future in Poor Dad and it was a loud wake up call

The book fully-resonated with me. Kiyosaki's tale of his two fathers: his biological dad (Poor Dad) and his father's childhood best friend, Mike (Rich Dad) and how both fathers achieved success in different ways highlighted which financial way made more sense.

Poor Dad is a hard worker, who has a lot of good ideas and good intentions, but most of his decisions often clash with his boss. Even his decision to run against his former boss in the mayoralty race, lost him, not just the election, but his livelihood as well.

I knew that path was parallel to where I was headed and it didn't bode well for Poor Dad. I certainly didn't want to end up like him.

The realization made an impact in me. I knew that I had to take immediate action so I could change my future. I knew that I had to start my own business in order to provide for my family.

So in this case, I knew my role model has to be someone whom I can relate to and shift my focus on a role model whom I can emulate to be successful. I believe that is Rich Dad.

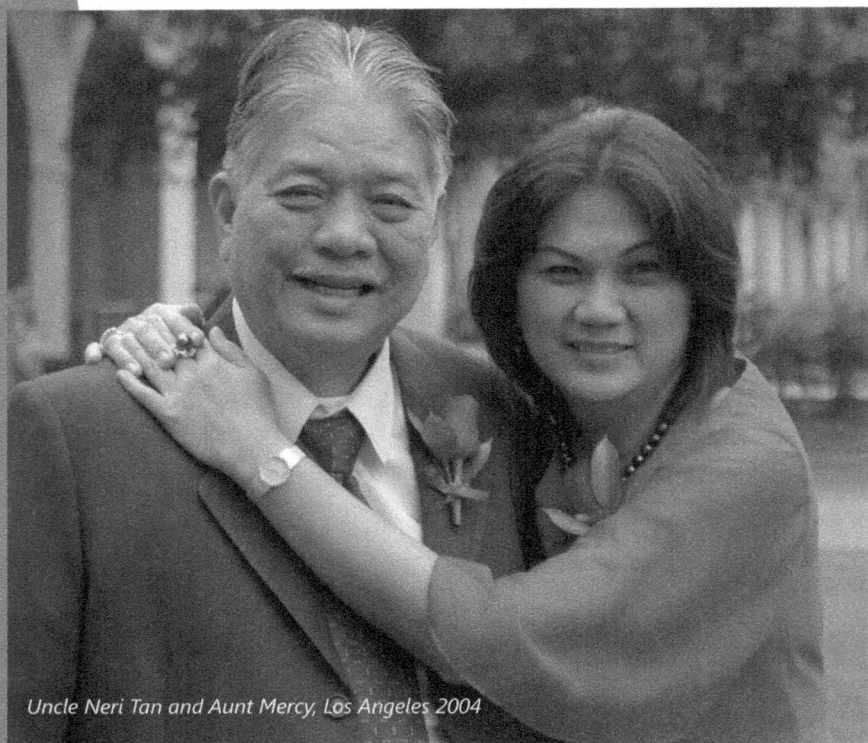

Uncle Neri Tan and Aunt Mercy, Los Angeles 2004

You must have had heroes or idols while growing up. People who you look up to because you admire their way of thinking or doing things. You look up to them because they create good results wherever they go. It may be your dad, your mom, your big brother or sister, your grade school teacher, your doctor, or whomever you see you'd aspire to be when you grow up. For me, it was my Uncle Neri.

I consider him as one of my best uncles. Uncle Neri was among the few people who genuinely wanted to help me succeed in business. He's a great mentor.

When I was struggling to stabilize M&L, the first company I worked with, Uncle Neri would always string me along to his sales calls. This widened my network of clients. He introduced me to some of his major customers like Nestle Philippines. My first sale to Nestle Philippines was only six pairs of rubber gloves which I had to deliver to Cabuyao, Laguna from Makati. Although the value was little, to me it felt like I just made a million bucks.

Uncle Neri once pitched the idea to start my own business, but at that time, I was very much occupied with the challenge of stabilizing what I started that I never entertained the idea. Establishing the company I co-founded challenged me so I never thought of leaving it. But Uncle Neri's reminder was at the back of my mind--it never left me. Finally Uncle Neri's calling won. I started preparing for my startup business, however, Uncle Neri didn't see it come to fruition.

In 2004, Uncle Neri died after being caught in a middle of a shootout between the police and armed robbers in Valenzuela. It was a really sad time for my family.

I was really affected by the incident. I could not help but think that life is so short. In just an instant, it can be taken away just like that. Everything suddenly seemed uncertain. You have no way of knowing if you can live through tomorrow or if there's even a tomorrow to look forward to.

I thought of my three kids: four-year-old twins, Hannah and Miles, and Daryl who's barely two years old then. What would happen to my kids if I were taken away just like my uncle? I became anxious. At that point, I knew God was sending me a message. I heard it loud and clear. Everything became crystal clear since then.

These events in my life weren't just coincidences. I believe these were signs for me to take the next step to build the life that I wanted for me and my family.

Heart and soul. My kids are my inspiration.

Tough times don't last. Tough teams do.
Blessing of the 2nd Blade office in Sheridan, Mandaluyong City with Chairman Emeritus Fidel Y. Tan (4th from left)

First, when I met Robert Kiyosaki, I knew that I had to fire my boss and start working on my dream. I needed to follow Rich Dad and invest in my family's future.

Second, the death of my Uncle made me realize there might be no tomorrow. If I don't start my own business now, then when? I was racing against time.

It was a huge wakeup call and it set me on a mission. Inspired by this epiphany, I set out to start something. I had to be clear of what I wanted so I decided to start with three objectives.

One, it should be something that is not in conflict with my previous employer. Two, it should be something that I can capitalize on my expertise, and three, it needs to have a higher chance of success.

Were there any risks holding me back? None. Holding on to the premise that I have only today to live, eliminated all the fears, doubts, and concerns I had. It also allowed me to focus on the task at hand.

PITSTOP ○

If you want to be successful, find a person who has achieved the results you want and copy what they do and you'll achieve the same results.

—Tony Robbins, American businessman and life success coach

Steve Jobs once said, "If today were the last day of my life, would I want to do what I am about to do today?' And whenever the answer has been `No' for too many days in a row, I know I need to change something."

I admire Steve Jobs for saying that; it's the same belief that my wife and I adhere to.

What if every day were your last? So much weight goes into that question. Knowing you're going to die makes life meaningful because it compels you to be at your best. You know you have to do that one thing that could make you happy. Do things that are worth your while. Do things which make the people around you feel loved. Do things that will have an impact on your surroundings. You want to cross out everything you have on your bucket list because you have realized that life is short. You consciously try to catch every moment, savoring it, so when you die, you know you have done everything.

My wife and I started to live every moment as if it were our last. We started living in the present. We seize the day and take the conscious effort to act on what we want to accomplish so we can secure our future. It is about making every day meaningful to improve the odds of success in the future. As they say, live in the present and the future will take care of itself.

So grab hold of what you thought was once out of reach, and in the process you will learn that nothing is out of reach. When you know it's your last day, you have no reason to fear or to worry. Anything is possible.

More often than not, successful individuals often look up to other people who 'made it' or those people who have been successful in the similar field they once wished to enter.

To emulate or to model after successful individuals helps shorten the learning curve because you already have a blueprint to follow. It will help you to avoid common mistakes and pitfalls. It will help you apply the necessary steps and strategies that have helped your role model succeed. Bottom line, it's easier to follow a path to success that is tried and tested.

So it only makes sense to find good role models, persons or individuals who have achieved success that you wish to achieve. And the role models you pick should reflect what you deem as important.

For example, you might have picked late Apple co-founder Steve Jobs as a role model because he's a genius or because of his business acumen. I personally consider Jobs as one of my role models because he was a visionary and he executed his vision in belief that he was paving the way for the future. He was passionate about his work and a hard worker—things that I admire and I value. His qualities reinforce my beliefs and these qualities influenced how I wanted to accomplish my goals.

There are plenty of good role models out there, but only a few can be your mentor. If your role model is accessible, for me that's a plus, the more you can learn and follow what his or her daily life is. The advantage of getting an accessible role model is that you get a glimpse of their day-to-day routine, which I believe you can learn more from.

A role model can offer advice and the how-to's, but a mentor can give you an opportunity to observe their thought patterns and what actions stem from those thoughts. My Uncle Neri showed me how to go about business just by allowing me to observe him while he's working. Tagging me along to every sales call he had for the day showed me how he dealt with clients—how he treats them, how he talks to them, how he makes decisions, how he closes deals—all of which a role model who you don't have access to can't teach you.

When choosing a role model, it should be someone who has faced and conquered the same challenges you are facing. Someone relatable, who you see yourself at a certain point in your life. Their early struggles could be similar or close to what you're going through at a particular point in your career or what you're trying to achieve. For someone with limited capital, a millionaire who has successfully put up a shoe business using money he saved up from doing odd jobs would be a great resource instead of a multimillionaire who inherited his million to put up his successful coffee chain.

If you are still looking for a role model, then you are at the early stages of trying to achieve something. It's best to learn how that person started out. How did they get into that business or trade. What his background is in the industry he entered. Make a research on his beginnings and see how you can copy his way of life so you can overcome the challenges you are facing and achieve the same results.

"The only impossible journey
is the one you never begin."
-Anthony Robbins

PITSTOP ⬤

I think I can!

—The Little Engine That Could

A good role model must possess self-efficacy. According to psychologist Albert Bandura, self-efficacy is one's belief in his or her ability to succeed in specific situations or accomplish a task. One's sense of self-efficacy can play a major role in how one approaches goals, tasks, and challenges.[12]

Positive role models believe in themselves. It's not just confidence, but it's the belief in one's capacity to rise up to any given situation or challenge to produce specific results to achieve a goal.

[12] Kendra Cherry, "Self-Efficacy: ___ In Yourself Matters," *VeryWell.com*, June 22, 2016, https://www.verywell.com/what-is-self-effica___ ___essed April 23, 2017)

One example is business mogul, television personality, and now President of the United States of America Donald Trump a.k.a. The Donald. Trump is known to have engineered the biggest financial turnaround in history.

Trump was quoted saying, "In the early 1990s, I owed billions of dollars and many people thought I was finished. I refused to give in to the negative circumstances and I never lost faith in myself. I didn't believe I was finished even when the newspapers were saying so. I refused to give up. Defeat is not in my vocabulary."

Henry Ford, a man who forever changed the automobile industry, wasn't deterred by bumps on the road when a couple of his businesses failed. Ford possessed self-efficacy and famously put it, "Whether you believe you can or can't, you are right."

Thus a positive role model is confident with a heart for the task at hand. Bandura enlists the following traits of someone who possesses self-efficacy.

PEOPLE WITH A STRONG SENSE OF SELF-EFFICACY
View challenging problems as tasks to be mastered
Develop deeper interest in the activities in which they participate
Form a stronger sense of commitment to their interests and activities
Recover quickly from setbacks and disappointments

PEOPLE WITH A WEAK SENSE OF SELF-EFFICACY
Avoid challenging tasks
Believe that difficult tasks and situations are beyond their capabilities
Focus on personal failings and negative outcomes
Quickly lose confidence in personal abilities[13]

So if you find the right role model who has the right recipe for success then you're well on your way to achieving your dream. ◀▷

JUMPSTART

- Reinforce your beliefs through daily positive thoughts.
- Find not just a role model, but a mentor who can teach you how to achieve success.
- Define the success you desire and find role models who struggled and surpassed the same challenges you are facing.
- A positive role model is someone who has a strong sense of self-efficacy.

---

[13] Cherry, "Self-Efficacy," https://www.verywell.com/what-is-self-efficacy-2795954 (accessed April 23, 2017)

The secret to being
Lucky
all the time

Success is composed of 5% inspiration and 95% perspiration (foundation and hard work). I truly believe that everything happens for a reason. There are no coincidences. Sometimes good things fall apart to give way for better things to come.

"Luck" should be defined as being prepared when opportunities arise. Although "luck" can make things run smoother, nothing beats a strong foundation, a well-thought out business plan, experience, discipline, and hard work. One needs to take action to fulfill their dreams, otherwise dreams will remain just that—dreams.

> **PITSTOP** ⬤
>
> *The grass is always greener where you water it.*
> **—Robertson Sy Tan,**
> **ThatGuyInRed.com**

*E*ver come across your Facebook feed and you see your college friend post a photo of himself with the caption "ATM Paris #blessed #grateful #travel" and you say to yourself, 'How come he's so lucky?'. Then you rationalize that he's been that lucky ever since because way back in college, his parents were overseas workers so they already had the money. No wonder he can travel. He's lucky. He was born lucky. Maybe.

But is luck everything about fate? Superstition? Or can luck be changed? Why are there some people luckier than others? Why are there people blessed with good fortune? Were there times you blame your lack of success on bad luck? Do you blame your luck or the lack thereof when you fail a test or fail a job interview? Do you sometimes ask yourself, "Why does it always happen to me?"

Merriam-Webster defines luck as a force that brings good fortune or adversity; the things that happen to a person

USS Midway, San Diego Air Craft Carrier Museum

because of chance; the accidental way things happen without being planned.

Our belief in luck may be traced back to our ancestors. As the species with higher thinking, humans have created beliefs to make sense of random life-changing tragic events, hence, superstition was born.

Throughout history people of different cultures from different times have lucky objects that mean a lot to them personally, objects almost universally believed to bring good luck. There are a wide array of objects, numbers, symbols, plants, and animal life that are revered in different cultures. The significance of each symbol is rooted in either folklore, mythology, esotericism, religion, tradition, necessity, or a combination thereof. [14]

The start of the New Year is always believed to be the best time to change one's luck. It's the time when everyone turns to the lucky charms or feng shui experts with the hope to reverse their fortunes and be lucky all year long.

---

[14] "Lucky symbols," *Wikipedia*, https://en.wikipedia.org/wiki/List_of_lucky_symbols (accessed February 2017)

Many believe it's an auspicious day to try out your luck. New Years mark a time of newly found happiness and a clean slate. For many who are celebrating New Years, it is their opportunity to learn from the prior year and make positive changes in their life. The reasoning behind New Years traditions and superstitions is that the first day of the year sets precedent for the following days.

Although I honor the traditions and beliefs that are brought down to me by my ancestors, I believe most of the time we make our own "luck". As some feng shui masters always say, these feng shui symbols and beliefs only serve as guides, we are the masters of our fate.

> ## PITSTOP ⬤
>
> *I am the master of my fate:*
> *I am the captain of my soul.*
>
> **—Invictus, William Ernest Henley**

When I was appointed President and CEO in 1991, the company I came into was at its lowest point—like a dying

One for all, all for One. In solidarity with the plight of my company, I volunteered to receive a peso check as monthly salary until I see signs of a turnaround.

patient in an Intensive Care Unit just waiting for his time. I vividly remember that day I held the company's passbook in my hands. The company's bank account contained less than Php 70,000.

It was disheartening, but I believed in what I was doing and was totally committed to turn the situation around. In my commitment to keep this company alive, I was willing to put my money where my mouth was. I was willing to get a monthly salary of one peso. That's right—a peso. I said I'm willing to be paid this much amount until the company sees signs of a turnaround, and our company treasurer reluctantly obliged.

With a lot of prayers and sheer hard work, I was able to turn the company around after four months. Consistent repeat sales started to come in and with an equally committed team, the company soon developed into a well-oiled machine. The company became stable the following year.

Rising up. After two years, the company was able to survive the crisis. Our company received an award for Outstanding Performance at the 3M Distributor Awards.

Within just two years after taking over, the company was as stable as a rock. The company didn't just survive one crisis after another, instead it thrived even when times were really bad. I dedicated so much of my life to this company that I spent 20 years of my productive life there. I loved it so much so that I even named my kids, twins, after the company and its products: Hannah (Hanns) and Miles (Miles&Levels).

My twins Hannah and Miles, 2004

So was "luck" just on my side for having successfully turned a company around? Simply random circumstance? Was it divine intervention? Or can we create good luck for ourselves?

Everything happens for a reason. When you pray for success, God provides opportunities to be successful. He blessed me with courage to take on this challenge at that stage of my life. He was also preparing me for bigger obstacles in my future. I believe it's God's way.

As I've said before, success lies in one's attitude. Good luck comes from action. Bad luck comes from inaction. All it takes is nothing more than but a concerted effort to change one's outlook to change one's so-called "luck".

The majority of people do this without realizing it. People attribute the occurrence of positive and negative events in their lives and perceive favorable events that occur repeatedly against the odds as good luck and when things take a turn for the worst it is deemed as bad luck.

As thanksgiving, our company celebrated our success by giving back. White Cross, San Juan City, 2008

Do you notice a pattern here? This pattern of thinking that fortune and misfortune are attributed to external factors that seem beyond one's control has an effect on your abilities to take charge of your life. It limits your ability to create true change and relieves you of responsibility to take control of events in your life, and becomes your 'escape goat' for failure.

With this mindset, you lose the chance to bring about any change in your life, and this cycle will keep on repeating until you take the wheel and steer your path towards success.

● ● ●

To test the theory that luck is more of a skill rather than random chance, psychologist Dr. Richard Wiseman studied how lucky and unlucky people think and behave. After three years of intensive interviews and experiments with over 400 volunteers, Wiseman arrived at an astonishing conclusion: "Luck" is something that can be learned.

Wiseman also pointed out that personality tests of 'unlucky' people indicated more tense and anxious in general than people who are considered 'lucky.' Anxiety disrupts people's ability to notice the unexpected. In one of his experiments, Wiseman asked subjects to watch a moving dot in the center of a computer screen. Without warning, large dots would occasionally be flashed at the edges of the screen. Nearly all participants noticed these large dots. The experiment was then repeated with a second group of people, who were offered a large financial reward for accurately watching the center dot. This time, people were far more anxious about the whole situation. They became very focused on the center dot and over a third of them missed the large dots when they appeared on the screen.[15]

[15] Robert Wiseman, "Be Lucky – It's an Easy Skill to Learn," *The Telegraph*, www.telegraph.co.uk/technology. (accessed February 2017)

PITSTOP

Unlucky people often fail to follow their intuition when making a choice, whereas lucky people tend to respect hunches. Lucky people are interested in how they both think and feel about the various options, rather than simply looking at the rational side of the situation. I think this helps them because gut feelings act as an alarm bell - a reason to consider a decision carefully.

Unlucky people tend to be creatures of routine. They tend to take the same route to and from work and talk to the same types of people at parties. In contrast, many lucky people try to introduce variety into their lives. For example, one person described how he thought of a colour before arriving at a party and then introduced himself to people wearing that colour. This kind of behaviour boosts the likelihood of chance opportunities by introducing variety.

Lucky people tend to see the positive side of their ill fortune. They imagine how things could have been worse. In one interview, a lucky volunteer arrived with his leg in a plaster cast and described how he had fallen down a flight of stairs. I asked him whether he still felt lucky and he cheerfully explained that he felt luckier than before. As he pointed out, he could have broken his neck.[16]

—Dr. Richard Wiseman, Psychologist

"A decade ago, I set out to investigate luck. I wanted to examine the impact on people's lives of chance opportunities, lucky breaks, and being in the right place at the right time. After many experiments, I believe that I now understand why some people are luckier than others and that it is possible to become luckier." said Dr. Richard Wiseman.

---

[16] Robert Wiseman, "The Luck Factor," *RobertWiseman.com*, http://www.richardwiseman.com/resources/The_Luck_Factor.pdf. (accessed February 2017)

PITSTOP

Most people lose the ability to see silver linings even though they are always there above us almost every day.

—Matthew Quick,
The Silver Linings Playbook

In a way, luck could have been responsible for some of the world's greatest successes. If luck comes in the form of a series of fortunate events like opportunities or lucky breaks, then success is inevitable.

In his book, Outliers, Malcolm Gladwell cites that having talent and being hard working has something to do with success, but some people do have the luck or opportunity. He cites Bill Gates as an example.

● ● ●

"Practice isn't the thing you do once you're good. It's the thing you do that makes you good." Gladwell shows how Gates accumulated his 10,000 hours while in middle and high school in Seattle thanks to a series of nine incredibly fortunate opportunities—ranging from the fact that his private school had a computer club with access to (and money for) a sophisticated computer, to his childhood home's proximity to the University of Washington, where he had access to an even more sophisticated computer. "By the time Gates dropped out of Harvard after his sophomore year to try his hand at his own computer software company, he'd been programming practically nonstop for seven consecutive years. He was way past 10,000 hours." Yes, Gates is obviously brilliant, but Gladwell concludes, without the lucky breaks he had as a kid, he never could have had the opportunity to fulfill the true potential of that brilliance. How many similarly brilliant people never get that opportunity? [17]

● ● ●

[17] Jason Zengerle, "Geek Popstar," *New York Magazine,* November 9,2008, http://nymag.com/arts/books/features/52014. (accessed February 2017)

PITSTOP ⬤

It is not the brightest who succeed... Nor is success simply the sum of the decisions and efforts we make on our own behalf. It is, rather, a gift. Outliers are those who have been given opportunities—and who have had the strength and presence of mind to seize them.

—*Outliers*, Malcolm Gladwell

Again, it is about the attitude. Raising awareness on the new possibilities and acting upon them creates good luck. Just like in the principles of feng shui which encourages the transformation of one's physical environments into energized, harmonious spaces that flow freely so chi or energy can flow freely and create good luck. Acting upon something creates energy which flows to all aspects of your life, thus creating more chance opportunities in finding better luck.

When good fortune befalls on you, remember it's because you seized the moment.

It is not wrong to believe in luck, but don't let it run your life. Enough well-thought-out decisions and hard work will surely allow more "good luck" to follow you around. Repeating these actions will certainly create the kind of luck you need to succeed.

This simple shift in perspective and realignment of attitude can be highly empowering. I never relied on luck. I relied on my efforts, and my gut to follow through the decisions and calculated timing I made. I did, however, prayed for guidance to humble myself to make decisions that are good and righteous.

I'm fastidious, pro-active, and eager. These proved to be the winning formula to make my dreams come true. If you continue to be positive, your efforts will be rewarded as mine were when I put up my business.

Challenges are unavoidable in life, but those who consider themselves makers of their own luck set themselves up for success and happiness. Positive thinking opens the gates for more possibilities and sets you up to a different level. A mind shift can help you reach goals you only dreamed of before. As the tagline of a vitamin company states, "What the mind can conceive, the body can achieve." It's guaranteed, and you don't even have to take a pill.

Being able to look at the bright side of things despite misfortune, will encourage more "luck" to come your way. Luck may be a matter of chance, and some people may be more blessed, but everyone can find a silver lining only if you allow yourself to look past the dark clouds.

Pula o Puti. Kapuso o Kapamilya. Jollibee o McDo. Lahat nagsama-sama. Para sa Milers Give Back.

PITSTOP ⬤

Luck? I don't know anything about luck. I've never banked on it, and I'm afraid of people who do. Luck to me is something else: Hard work— and realizing what is opportunity and what isn't.

—Lucille Ball, actress comedienne on luck

So if you're reading this book now, think about how it came into your hands. Is it by luck? Will you take the time to learn something to improve yourself? Either way, it's a very fortunate event. ◆◆

● ● ●

JUMPSTART

- Everything happens for a reason. There are no coincidences.
- "Luck" should be defined as being prepared when opportunities arise.
- Unlucky people often fail to follow their intuition when making a choice, whereas lucky people tend to respect hunches. Lucky people are interested in how they both think and feel about the various options, rather than simply looking at the rational side of the situation.
- Positive thinking opens the gates for more possibilities and sets you up to a different level.

Sometimes, the most Expensive advice you may receive is

Free Advice

On your road to achieving your goals, you need to be careful in screening the ideas and thoughts being handed to you. Not all friends or relatives have your best interest in mind. Some may want to keep things the way they are rather than see you make progress.

Do not cloud your mind with negative thoughts. The road towards success may sometimes be bumpy. Choose your friends wisely. Listen to those who encourage you rather than discourage, because they might affect your future.

5

"Create the highest grandest vision possible for your life, because you become what you believe." -Oprah Winfrey
Blade Auto Cycle Show 2006, Glorietta Activity Center, Makati City

*I*n the journey to success or life in general, you will encounter so many insights from various people. Always be careful where you get them and who you listen to. It's important to screen out which advice is actually worthwhile, and which is not helpful. According to Amy Morin, author of *13 Things Mentally Strong People Don't Do*, there are three people whose advice you should consider.

One, **people who care about you**. I think it's good sense to listen to people who truly care about you, because they have your best interest in mind. It may be a parent who can pass on their wisdom to you, or a best friend who would be willing to tell the truth even if it hurts. Advice from these people is not self-serving; they are clearly offered to help you to succeed, and also provide different perspectives when you need guidance.

Two, **people with clear expertise**. Just like looking for a role model or a mentor, seek out advice from people who are successful and have overcome those challenges that you are facing at the moment. Look for individuals who have proven expertise in the field or industry or business you want to enter. You will learn more from the experts since they understand the obstacles you face.

Do it big. Do it right. Do it with style.
Wellington Soong, distributor of luxury vehicles.

Full speed ahead. With automotive journalist and CNN Philippines' Service Road host James Deakin.

Three, **people who use your services**. Differentiate between constructive criticism and baseless criticism to simply tear down your work. Listen to feedback from people you serve. These customers and clients are at the receiving end of your business and they know firsthand which works and which does not. Users' experience and their feedback will help you improve your business. Keep feedback in context and don't let the negative ones drown out your ideas and beliefs. Of course, do so and screen out the trolls and bashers' comments while you're at it.

The quote above relates to the law of averages, which states that the result of any given situation is the average of all outcomes. Studies have shown that the relationships we keep impact our way of thinking, self-esteem, and decisions. So if you keep hanging around with people who do nothing but whine all day, contradict every good idea you come up with, or sulk all day — then chances are you absorb these attitudes as well.

Previous chapters discussed that a positive attitude is a must to reach your full potential and achieve success. So how are you going to achieve your goals if there are negative blocks that hamper your success? If you say that you've removed and ignored all your bashers and toxic people in your life, then you have done well.

beware of people who pretend to be a friend but is actually a rival

Most of us are no strangers to people who constantly pull us down, but I'm not just talking about bullies who make life difficult for us in school or manipulative people who are just downright mean and play with your emotions and guilt. Sometimes friends and even family members constantly criticize and discourage you, instead of encouraging you.

True, there are times that only friends and family can tell you the bitter truth to help you and see the reality. But there are those who constantly bring you down. Social media has coined the word 'frenemy' as a person who pretends to be your friend, but is actually a rival.

Reflect on your past and write down instances in your life when a particular friend or family member whom you've always sought for advice or comments (or someone who gave unsolicited advise). Did they commonly have something negative to say or discourage you from starting a new venture or direction in life?

List down particular life events or life-changing moments and the people who discouraged you from pursuing something. These are the people who, when you had a glorious moment or success, were not really happy for you; And when you fail, they add more insult to injury instead of cheering you up.

Life is too short to have people around you who make it more difficult to succeed or to be happy. They can be likened to 'kontrabidas' (bad guys) in a television soap opera. People who overtly make your life miserable and smile at your demise. People who are unaware of their negative impact on those around them and derive satisfaction on pushing other people's buttons. Who needs the added stress? Stress has been shown to have a lasting, negative impact on the brain.

Negativity of any kind—financial, familial, or job-related—create more intense and often prolonged negative emotions that ultimately result in stress that taxes our mental resources.[18]

● ● ●

So how do you spot these negative individuals? Here are six types of people you should stay away from:

The Vampire. A mythological creature who sucks the blood out of its victims turning them into vampires or killing them. This type of person drains you of your energy and emotions. They suck the life out of you, and you feel more tired and more stressed. It doesn't stop there, as misery loves company. They rejoice if you're unhappy or in trouble; they find consolation if you both share negative views.

The Narcissist. Believes that the whole universe revolves around them, and expects everyone to adjust to their needs. This person expects much more from you than they are willing to give. This person expects compliance and takes advantage of other people.

---

[18] Travis Bradberry and Jean Greaves, "Emotional Intelligence 2.0" (San Diego: TalentSmart 2009), p.230.

If you discuss your experiences with them, they will always inject a story which will take the spotlight away from you. This person always steals your thunder whenever something good happens to you, managing to upstage you. Sometimes they even get a good laugh at your expense.

The Gossip. Always beware of the presence of this type of person. Be careful of what you say around them. This individual can't resist a good story and will surely rat it out to anybody. They love the juicy details of your life and talk about it to other people, most of the time weaving wild tales of your personal life.

The Doubter. He finds every reason or excuse not to support you. This person has millions of reasons why you shouldn't go through with that new business and will not support or encourage you. This 'friend' doesn't believe you have it in you to go through with a project or endeavor. They remind you of your failures and challenge your competence.

The Envious. This little green-eyed monster is not genuinely happy for you when you tell him or her of some good news or that exciting new project you are working on. Every time you succeed at something or have good news, this friend acts distant or dismissive. You always find it difficult or awkward to break any good news or anything you're happy with when you're with this type of person.

The Critic. The know-it-all : This person gives valid insights to the field you want to be in, yet they are not exactly experts in the field. This person kills your confidence and throws you off the balance. This 'friend' thinks they are always right and if you attempt to prove them wrong you won't hear the end of it.

Remember, you don't have to heed these people. You can always minimize interaction if you cannot sever ties, especially if they are kin.

Similar to how celebrities "ignore" bashers. Choose your battles and don't get all defensive or worked up worrying about a harsh critic. Learn to tune those people out. The best way to shut these haters up is to not let them win by justifying your decisions to the point of arguing with them. Sometimes the secret to winning an argument is to just keep quiet about it.

● ● ●

WHAT WOULD YOU DO? IF THIS WAS YOUR LAST DAY ON EARTH

Here we grow. The ever-growing family of Bladers at the Thanksgiving Party in March, 2014

PITSTOP ⬤

Do not seek praise. Seek criticism.

—It's Not How Good You Are, It's How Good You Want to Be, Paul Arden

All successful people know that, in order to increase your wins, you've also got to increase your losses.[19] And as important as surrounding yourself with positive and supportive people to help you succeed, it's also important to have critics.

Remember the saying, 'please all and you will please none'? You can't make everyone happy. Although you may be doing the very best you can to make your customers happy, there will be those who won't be. There will always be those people who will not like what you do, it can sometimes mean they are not your market or they are trying to tell you something that you ought to improve on. Although positive feedback helps you feel good about yourself, it is actually the negative ones that brings about progress, specifically constructive feedback. So if you have produced a pleasantly

If you really want something, believe in yourself.
Go for it because life is short.

---

[19] Aimee Groth, "You're The Average of The Five People You Spend The Most Time With," *Business Insider*, July 24,2014, http://www.businessinsider.com/jim-rohn-youre-the-average-of-the-five-people-you-spend-the-most-time-with-2012-7 (accessed February 2017)

acceptable piece of work, you will have just proved to yourself that it's good simply because others have said so. Not bad but then it's not great either. Try to ask questions like, 'What's wrong with it? How can I make it better?'. In this way, you are more likely to get a truthful, critical answer. You may even get an improvement on your idea.

If there's anything you need to know about success is that it isn't always easy. There will always be people who will make life difficult. Among them are people whose goal is to make your life miserable. But sometimes, in a twist of fate, they can be reason you succeed. Because in some situations, their constant belittling can help you develop mental toughness which is key to overcoming so many hurdles in life.[20]

[20] Paul Arden, "It's Not How Good You Are, It's How Good You Want To Be," (London: Phaidon Press, 2003), p.26-27.

Mental toughness is key to becoming successful. It is how an individual responds to adversity or extreme situations and be able to bounce back. In his book *Rebounders*, Rick Newman notes that, "Setbacks can be a secret weapon. They often teach vital things you'll never learn in school, on the job, or from others."

What's great about mental toughness is that it's a skill. You can learn it. Tackling problems and setbacks help you to innovate and in time grow accustomed to managing a crisis. These critics can be the ones that keep you on your toes and help you think and act accordingly to every problem instead of resting on your laurels. ◄►

JUMPSTART

- It's important to screen out which advice is actually worthwhile, and which isn't helpful.

- Relationships can influence our attitudes and decisions. Let go of toxic relationships. If severing ties is not an option, especially if it's a family member, firmly minimize interactions with them.

- Tune out bad feedback and focus on constructive criticism.

- Your critics are also those who test your perseverance and mental toughness.

SOMETIMES, THE MOST EXPENSIVE ADVICE YOU MAY RECEIVE IS FREE ADVICE

Remember your roots.
Tree planting at Nuvali, Laguna 2016
in celebration of Blade's 12th anniversary

BLADE
AUTO CENTER
September 17, 2016
500 trees

Be Willing to Lose the Battle in Order to Win the War.

In many cases, taking one step backward in order to move two steps forward may be the best option to consider. As long as you are focused on achieving your goals, and not let anything stand in your way. Pride may sometimes lead you to make wrong decisions, so be careful.

No matter how high up you are in the corporate ladder, you are still accountable to someone above you if you are not the owner. You will always be at the mercy of your superiors no matter how good your performance may be. In some cases, you cannot express your real opinion, even if it is for the good of the company, especially if it goes against the ideas of your boss. It's a reality for all who are employed. That reality was not something that sat well with me. Hence, the beginning of my mission to build my own company.

Blade First Snow Experience, Tokyo, 2017

Until you spread your wings, you'll never know how far you can fly. Bandang Blade - Motoring Music Festival 2017. A Philippines' first.

As a businessman and entrepreneur, I've learned so much from the industry. You must learn faster, improve every day, get back on your feet after every setback, learn from your mistakes, and take criticism graciously.

Sometimes, to get closer to the person you dream to be and become successful, you don't need to add more—you rather, you may have to give up something. Successful businessmen and entrepreneurs alike know that in order to increase your wins, you've also got to increase your losses.

You may have to give up some things to make way for the better. Maybe having to let go of some relationships—no, I'm not talking about friends on Facebook with whom you

have different political leanings, but the kind that won't help you achieve your desired results.

You might think that being appointed as President and CEO of a company is the pinnacle of success. Well in a way it is, but I have a different definition of success- to fulfill a lifelong dream. Although I loved my work and all that came with it, I knew that I had to give it up to achieve a higher level of success. The escalating conflict with my former boss increased the urgency for me to set a different career path. If you think it's annoying to go to work every day and hear your office mate rant all day, what more having to deal with a difficult boss? This led to my decision to let go of my position instead of clashing with my boss and burning bridges along the way.

PITSTOP

Someone once taught me that if you want something to happen in your life, you have to make room for it.

—Michael Tetterton, CEO Creative Lodging Solutions for Inc.com

The old adage, "No pain, no gain" can be summed up in one word- sacrifice. Individuals who are trying to lose weight know that to achieve a lean and strong body, they need to sacrifice eating anything that will slow down their progress: bread, sweets, processed foods, white sugar, white flour, fried food, etc.). They also know that you need to put in the work which means time and commitment.

To commit to a healthy lifestyle, you really don't need a lot, but you need to do less of the things that pack on the pounds. You need a healthy diet and physical activity – every single day. But to be successful in your weight loss endeavor, you must commit to doing it repeatedly every day, even if it's boring and routine. You have to sacrifice that late night movie so you can wake up early in the morning and fit in that morning workout. Sacrifices. You need to shun what's weighing you down to be your best self.

When you commit, you need to let go of the short term to make way for the long term. One classic example can be related to the habits of saving and spending money. Everyone knows the basics of saving money. You keep an amount to save for later spending. Most of us have money goals which we allot to spend for daily expenses, emergencies, and needs and wants. Of course, when we receive money, either earned or given as a gift, we think about what we want to spend our money on. We divide it into two categories: money we will spend now, a short-term goal and money we save for later spending, a long-term goal.

Short-term savings goal refers to money which you hope to have within a shorter length of time like in a few days, weeks, or months to buy or pay for something. It may be for new clothes, shoes, a movie, or simply having coffee with friends.

PITSTOP ⬤

I once had a partner who taught me to live by the phrase, "A lot of littles equal a lot." In life and business, it's not one big thing that creates lasting success; it's the summary of all of the little things that, done well and consistently over time, makes a company or product a winner.

—David Kalt is the founder of Reverb.com

Long-term savings goal refers to money which you hope to have for a longer period of time – a span of several months or years—to buy for things that are expensive like a trip with the family, a car, or a house.

Everyone also knows that if we save 20% of our salaries each month, we could save money that can be spent or saved for bigger things. So we forgo buying that venti coffee or splurging on those new watches to save up for a trip with the family. You may choose to get an insurance coverage or an education plan for the kids that can save you a substantial amount for a future event. The accumulation of the unspent money from your short-term savings goals will lead to achieving your long-term goal.

According to *Rich Dad Poor Dad* author Robert Kiyosaki, getting rich is about small steps leading to great wealth over time. It's having the power of vision, gratification, and compounding to make or break your dreams.

Kiyosaki also enumerated three qualities of the wealthy and the three qualities of the poor and how their money spending habits affect their wealth.

Families are like branches on a tree. We grow in different directions yet we remain as one.

Three qualities of the Wealthy

1. They maintain a long-term vision and plan. The study found that these people thought and planned for the long term and knew that they would ultimately achieve financial success by holding on to a dream or vision.

2. They believe in delayed gratification. Rather than get everything they wanted right now, these people were willing to make short-term sacrifices to gain long-term success.

3. They use the power of compounding in their favor. Income is re-invested to maximize gains.

Three qualities of the Poor

1. They have short-term vision. The poor have no vision of the long-term.

2. They have a desire for immediate gratification. Many are desperately seeking short-term answers because they have money problems today caused by consumer debt and lack of investments due to their uncontrolled desire for immediate gratification. They have the lifestyle of, "Eat, drink, and be merry."

3. They abuse the power of compounding. Instead of learning to invest, the poor lack good saving habits.[21]

So it's time to change that short-term mindset. Instead of focusing on doing things for the short term, you need to make those short-term goals that will serve as stepping stones to achieve your long-term goal. Your daily habits become you.

---

[21] Robert Kiyosaki, *"Three Qualities to Become Wealthy (And Three More to Become Poor),"* RichDad.com, http://www.richdad.com (accessed March 2017)

PITSTOP ⬤

...the best way to meet and exceed the expectations of our customers was to hire and train great people, we invested in employees.

**—Howard Schultz,
Starbucks chairman**

*Keep taking chances and have fun doing it.
Blade Auto Center in Megamall, Mandaluyong City*

Achieving our dreams
by helping others achieve theirs.
We work hard, we play hard.

We only have limited time, and can only do so much. That is why from the beginning, we set up Blade with a system as though we were operating franchise stores. The design is inspired by the way big fast food chains operate their stores. The crew will just have to follow the system. They do not need a college degree. The main qualification for hiring and maintaining staff was determined by their ability to follow procedures.

Only time can tell. In general, we believe that people are good and trustworthy. Sure, there may be some bad eggs in the basket, but most are inherently good. We trust our team with the store inventory, sales, and keys to the stores.

During one of my discussions with a student group, I was asked "Why do you trust your staff? Won't they cheat or steal from you?" My view is that we live in a society where people are given the benefit of the doubt. We treat our team well. We give them the proper compensation. We treat everyone with respect and try our best to help everyone reach their full potential. If you treat your team well, they will be motivated to do a good job and will develop a sense of commitment to the team.

There will surely be people who have ill-intents, and frankly, I think it is their loss. If you're part of a strong team which values its members, and you still set out to cheat or steal from your team, that's all on you. In the end, it's not the team who was short-changed. It's you.

As a leader, I have to be objective. If an employee fails to abide by the company policies even though he or she have been excellent all throughout his or her employment, he or she will not be excused from the repercussions of his or her actions.

I do not want to change the way I treat my team simply because I feel that I want to favor someone who has shown commitment yet bypassed some rules. The end doesn't justify the means. What about the 20 team members who weren't as exceptional performance-wise yet are committed and loyal? For me, it's a no-brainer. The team may have lost a valuable member, but there are still members who can be trained and have the good sense to abide by company policies.

● ● ●

> ## PITSTOP ⬤
>
> *Any successful entrepreneur knows that time is more valuable than money itself.*
>
> **—Richard Branson, Virgin Group**

It is true you can only be successful if you are productive with your time. If something is not worth your time be open to say, 'No.' Do you have a friend who always can't come to dinners or parties because he or she has to stay after work? Do you know a parent who can't go to his son's graduation because he needs to be at work? How about an OFW who can't go home for Christmas because they want to earn extra to be sent to their family back home? These people must sacrifice birthdays, occasions, and milestones because they are working for their family's futures.

Very successful entrepreneurs often must say 'No' to accomplish bigger things. We have to say 'No' to certain activities and demands from friends and family, sadly, because we need to attend to something more important that will increase our chances to accomplish those goals we've set. These goals require time. We don't bother with activities that won't lead us closer to our goals.

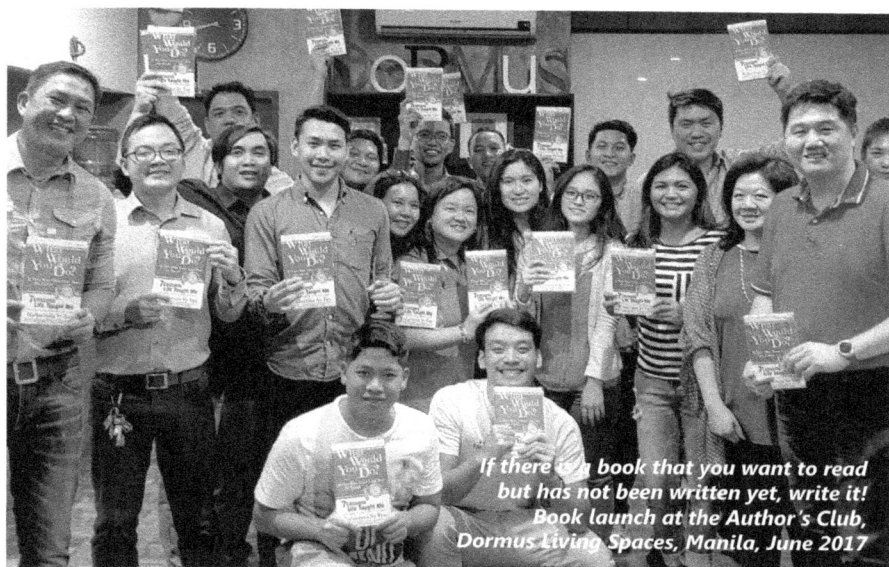

If there is a book that you want to read but has not been written yet, write it! Book launch at the Author's Club, Dormus Living Spaces, Manila, June 2017

We need to fit in as much work in the limited time we have—but usually at a price, because we know at the end it will be worth it. He who sacrifices greatly will attain highly.

PITSTOP ●

Some things are up to us, and some things are not up to us.

—Epictetus, Stoic philosopher

If you want to pursue business, you have to take some risk. Accept the fact that you can't control everything. If you put so much focus on conditions, it becomes counter productive and may be setting yourself up for disappointment. You're not competing against the market or the competition. You are competing against yourself. When you focus on conditions or the competition, you divert your focus to things you can't control.[22] As I've said before, I'm thankful for competition because if it weren't for them, I wouldn't be able to see what needs improvement.

It's a total waste of energy to focus on 'uncontrollables'. What you can control is your attitude and how you respond to ever changing conditions. The true test is how you successfully respond to these conditions and adapt in order to benefit from them.

Every sunrise is a reminder that life can be a new beginning.
Blade Auto Center, main office at Timog Ave., Quezon City, Philippines

It also means giving up the need to do everything. Successful people know that, in order to achieve their goals, they need to focus on one task and delegate the rest to other people. Be committed to put your attention to the Most Important Task (MIT) and let your people do other tasks that

---

[22] John Brubaker, "Don't Waste Focus," *Entrepreneur.com*, June 24, 2015, https://www.entrepreneur.com/article/247641(accessed March 2017).

the only constant thing is change and success depends on how you adapt to it

they are trained for. That's why you hire people who are better than you, so you can focus on the most important goal.

When we hire people, we trust them with our business. We train them and treat them well in hopes that they would also have the same passion and commitment towards the business. We don't have control over how our people will perform and respond to everyday challenges at work. We can't regulate the market landscape, but we can direct our responses to the changes and that's how we continue to innovate and improve the brand. The only constant thing is change and success depends on how you adapt to it.

PITSTOP ●

*If you do not change,
you can become extinct!*

**—Who Moved My Cheese,
Spencer Johnson**

A successful businessman is someone who never rests on his laurels. He is always on his toes, looking for ways to improve each day. A good work flow doesn't always mean that the business is going well and there's no need to change anything. It can be a false sense of security. Business has to be always dynamic and we can't afford to be stagnant. We need to keep up with our world.

A change in the workplace is a good thing because this is the time to look at key markers on how to make the business better. A loss in the workplace can be anything, like a loss of a valuable client or a key employee. It can be a loss of a major account which could impact your company's sales and profits. It could be what insurance companies call an 'Act of God' or events outside human control such as flood, fire, earthquakes, or major weather events. It can be mistakes in a business plan or marketing. It can also be the economy itself. Entrepreneurs must learn to take these losses and be able to recover.

A loss can help gain perspective. It is the best time to reevaluate, reassess, reinvent, and redefine the company's goals and strategies. This is an opportunity to weed out what works and what doesn't. It just means there is a need to change our attitudes and our way of thinking and better ourselves.

JUMPSTART

- Sacrifice much and you achieve much. Sacrifice greatly and you achieve highly.

- Let go of the short-term mindset. Always set short-term goals that will lead to accomplishing your long-term goal.

- Treat your employees well and they will treat your business well. It will also lessen your employee turnover rate.

- Time is gold. Be productive of your time.

- Don't sweat over the small stuff. Don't waste time thinking of what you can't control.

- Change is always good in business.

Have faith, He knows what He is doing

We can't always see where the road leads but God promises there's something better up ahead. We just have to trust Him.

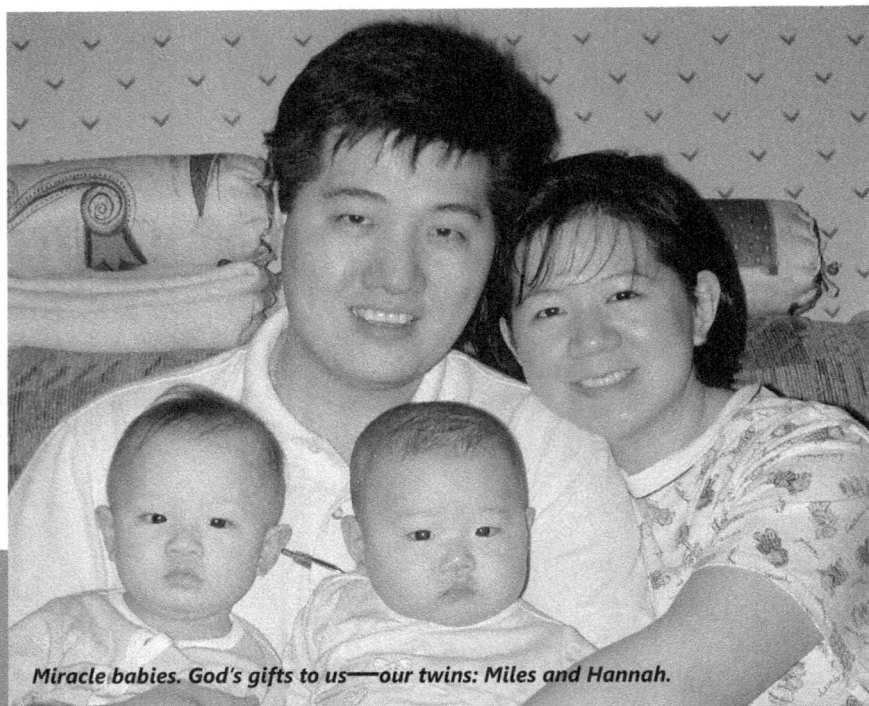

Miracle babies. God's gifts to us——our twins: Miles and Hannah.

rances and I have experienced God's grace first hand. We were praying to have a child. We had been childless since we got married in 1991.

Our faith in God was put to the test when we were informed that an unwed mother was ready to give up her baby for adoption. We were overjoyed about the prospect of becoming instant parents. Both of us had discussed and never stopped praying for some guidance and answers.

Choosing to adopt would have been the easy solution. There's an old Chinese belief that says, when you adopt a child, you will attract the universe to give you your own.

But was it God's will for us? After a few days of prayers, we decided that adoption wasn't for us. We believed that it would be unfair to adopt a child for the wrong reasons.

On our eighth anniversary, my Aunt Mely referred us to see a fertility doctor. We did and finally went through the medical procedure. Afterwards, I distinctly remember the doctor saying, "Science and medical advancement can only do so much. Now, we need to pray that what I had done will work." And it did. God, didn't just bless us with a child, He blessed us with twins! Praise God!

We were told by the doctor that with our condition, we would not be able to get pregnant without medical help. We accepted that. We prayed for a baby and were blessed with two. We were very happy.

Make a wish.
Daryl celebrating her first birthday.

About a year and a half later, Frances showed me the ultrasound printout. I was so surprised and extremely happy to learn she was pregnant with Daryl. We did not seek any medical help for this- she just came naturally!

You know the saying, "when it rains, it pours"? Well, after we welcomed Daryl into our family, our youngest daughter, Redd, came to our life. I guess everything will be right in God's time.

Studies have shown that highly successful people have a morning ritual before they start their work. These rituals help them become proactive and productive throughout the day. Remember the saying, 'The early bird gets the worm'? It doesn't only hold true for the bird, but for us humans too. The early morning provides fewer distractions, thus you can focus on a task more intently.

Aside from waking up early in the morning to utilize most of the morning hours, most successful entrepreneurs engage in some mindfulness activity. It may be in the form of an exercise routine, a quiet meditation, or saying a prayer- this practice helps to act as buffer before taking on the challenges of the day.

I start mine with a prayer. Prayer brings to focus all what I need to do for the day and my way of asking for spiritual help to guide my decisions throughout the day.

InspiRedd.
We welcomed Redd into our family in 2005.

Now, you don't need to be a Catholic or be religious to believe in God. Your personal relationship with a higher being is important. Prayer in a nutshell is about focus and discipline, traits that have great relevance to daily business performance. People of many religions who pray regularly use dedicated time and ritual to organize their thoughts and feelings. Those who do so daily find meditative value in clearing their mind and grounding their soul, so they can better deal with people in a strong, calm, and centered manner. Daily prayers give you the space to focus on what is really important and at the same time mentally and emotionally prepares you for whatever is coming your way, be it a challenge or opportunity. Knowing that whatever happens, you implore the blessings and protection of the Almighty God.

Celebrated Blade's 10th anniversary at the Asociacion De Damas De Filipinas child caring facility for abandoned, neglected, orphaned, foundling, and dependent

[23] Kevin Daum, "The Power of Prayer for Business," *Inc.com*, April 5, 2013, http://www.inc.com/kevin-daum/the-power-of-prayer-for-business.html (accessed March 2017)

Constant praying to my God has opened my eyes to my purpose every day. Through prayer, I am able to recognize the opportunities that help me reach my goals.

One such instance was during a swimming party I brought my kids to, which led to a chance encounter with Harley Sy of SM Malls. I took the opportunity to talk to him about my plans to start a business. I threw in a few ideas, and one of them was putting up a car accessories retail store. He told me that it is a niche unfilled and that it was a good direction to go . With that, my journey began.

As soon as I made the declaration, ideas started to pour in. Store images, designs, and merchandise all came in easily. But at every initial stage of putting up a business, there are labor pains that accompany it.

As we scouted for a potential location, the space at Karport, Fort Bonifacio attracted us. The space was small enough so as not to incur a big overhead, and the location is visible to motorists. The space is located in a strip wherein most of the tenants are, in one way or another, related to the car industry. It was perfect for what we had in mind.

After weeks of negotiations and trying to pinpoint an available space, we soon learned that our target space had been taken and that there were no more available spaces in Karport. Disappointed, we had to start looking elsewhere.

A setback such as this can be expected, but I wasn't discouraged. My calm and positive outlook brought about by my faith in God will always lead me to an open door and help me face challenges. I understand why some doors close. I believe God is faithful as I am to Him.

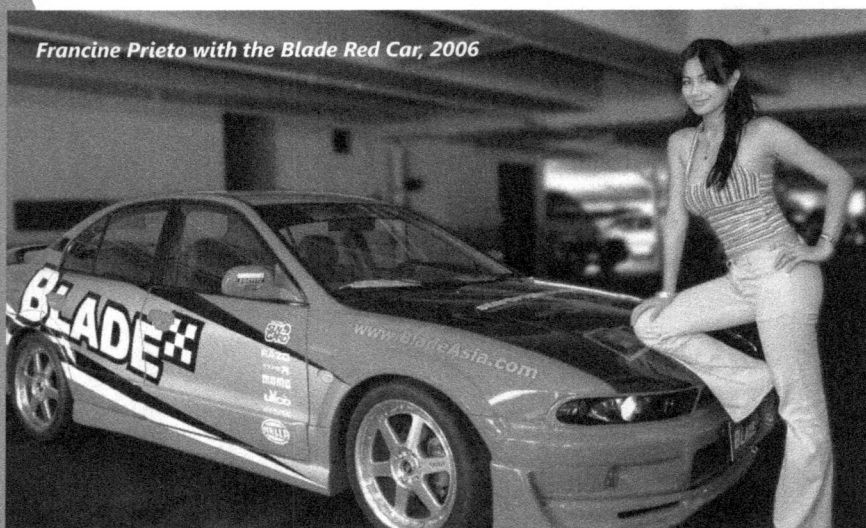

Francine Prieto with the Blade Red Car, 2006

Fresh. Blade is a new concept that invaded the retail market.

After being rejected at Karport, we learned that the Ayala Group was building a mall at Fort Bonifacio, not far from our target location. The new mall was being developed as the new shopping destination in the hottest zip code in the metro—Bonifacio Global City. The new mall (it became what is now Market! Market!) would house a department store, a supermarket, various food stalls and restaurants, market stalls selling the freshest produce, and of course, there would be hundreds of parking spaces.

Since we were starting a business at a time when the economy was bad and very few retail chains were expanding, this was a perfect opportunity for us. We applied for a space and were immediately accepted.

At that time, Blade Auto Center was the only one of its kind. An automotive retail store which adopted the boutique style store merchandising. Our brightly lit store, with its attractive show windows, was an instant hit. Mall operators liked our fresh concept so much that offers to put up stores in other malls started to come in.

When it rains, it pours. Blade Auto Center became a fast-rising star in the automotive retail market.

Looking back, I do believe that God pointed us to this direction so that we could expand as fast as we wanted. If we had been accepted at our originally planned location, our future may have been a lot different.

PITSTOP ⬤

Ask, and it shall be given you; seek, and ye shall find; knock, and it shall be opened unto you

—Matthew 7:7

Entrepreneurs want success for their business and by praying, we believe we can find success. Success driven individuals pray and meditate more often. It is so because it leads us to our purpose and live in accordance to God's will. Everyone has a unique imprint which needs to be shared to the world. The only time one can realize that gift is if one lives a life which is in alignment with ones' purpose. Prayer is a way to communicate our desires to God and to the universe. Through constant prayer, we sense that we are not alone. We feel a spiritual guidance that leads us to see and become open to opportunities and grace. We reinforce our desire to our sub-conscious self that we need to be diligent until we find what we are looking for. Knock and it shall be opened means be persistent in prayer. Our faith will lead us to God's answers and by faith will lead us to act in ways that is pleasing to Him.

PITSTOP ⬤

"When you come to God in Prayer, it is like a child talking to his Father, without any pretensions, acknowledging that He knows you more than yourself. And you surrendering your will for His because He has His best plans for you."

—Sam Liuson, Discipleship Group Leader, Christ's Commission Fellowship (CCF)

Prayer is very personal to me because it is not only my direct line to Him, but it is where I open up every aspect of my life to Him. Prayer has opened me to lots of things in my life, and taught me many lessons. It has taught me to be thankful of the things in my life which I thought were of little significance before, but in hindsight were a big part of how my life shaped up to be.

The daily struggles to test my patience were there to help me find ways to improve the little things that needed fixing. Prayer helped me act appropriately and do something with my time instead of worrying. It also helped me to appreciate not only the things that go my way, but for the things that made my early years difficult. If it weren't for those blocks and challenges, I wouldn't have had the toughness to face them and make those life-changing decisions.

The more I pray, the more my faith deepens, and the more I come to see how God has been faithful to me and His promises.

Sometimes all we need is a hand to hold and a heart to understand.

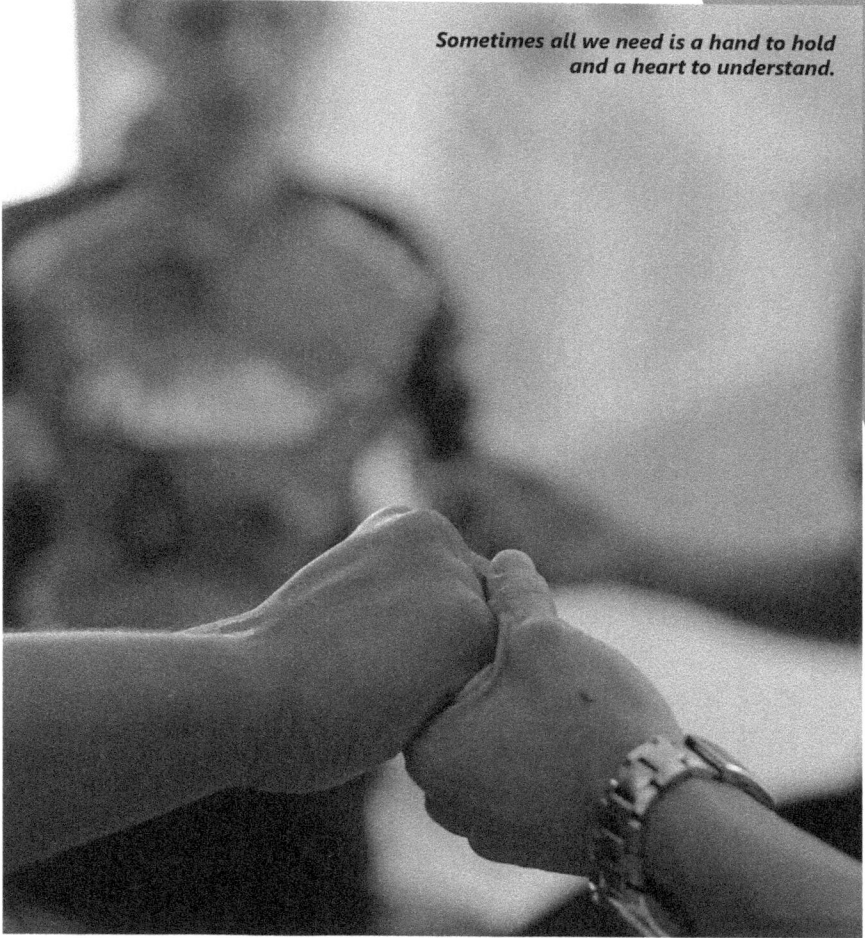

Prayer has also drawn me closer to people who pray and drawn me closer to Church. And in Church, I get to meet people to connect with and share my experiences, and we learn. Best of all, prayer has provided me a way to allow other people to pray for me as well. If you think about, it that's what

Church is for; everyone can pray for one another. And when other people pray for you, watch out, something big is about to happen.

And you think prayer has nothing to do with business? When I started this business, I knew it was ambitious. It was such a huge endeavor that delving into starting on my own was actually scary and daunting, but I knew I had to do it. I needed more than just capital. I possessed the will, the hard work ethic, and had support from all of my loved ones. I also knew I needed someone who's going to help me and push me to go through it all. I knew I needed God. I knew I had to pray for it. I knew I must have the faith to do it. And pray I did.

Giving thanks. We always remember where we come from and are grateful for what we have. Blade Thanksgiving Celebration 2016.

I recently read a study by the Harvard Business Review about how entrepreneurs are actually closer to God. A professor named Mitchell J. Neubert along with his Baylor University colleagues investigated the connection between faith and the propensity to start a business. They examined data from a survey from 1,714 U.S. adults about their religious habits. From that data, they gathered that entrepreneurs prayed more frequently than their non-entrepreneur counterparts. Interesting? There's more. Neubert and company also found that entrepreneurs pray several times a week. These people believe that God cares so much about them, that's why they talk to Him frequently. What's more, the researchers also found that entrepreneurs are also apt to worship with a congregation that encourages business activity. [24]

So we pray. We believe God cares about us that's why we talk to Him frequently.

---

[24] Mitchell J Neubert, "Entrepreneurs Feel Closer to God Than the Rest of Us Do," *Harvard Business Review*, October 2013 issue, https://hbr.org/2013/10/entrepreneurs-feel-closer-to-god-than-the-rest-of-us-do (accessed March 2017)

Paying it forward. With so much blessings come the responsibility to be a blessing to others and give back.

So what do I pray for? Everything. I pray for good health. I pray that I close that big deal. I pray for my family's welfare. I pray that my wife and I will live to see our kids fulfill their dreams. I pray that Blade will be around for a long time to help people. I pray my employees will get it right and remember everything that I tell them. I pray that my new marketing campaign will work. I pray something will go wrong with my competitors' marketing campaign. Just kidding. (I'm thankful for my competitors, because they keep us on our toes and challenge us to come up with bigger and better ideas each time.).

But as I grow into my faith, my prayers have also changed. I just don't see God as someone to ask for things for. Believe me, I asked so many things from Him and almost always I don't get what I want. Instead He gives me what I need to get what I want. You may have encountered this kind of talk lots of times and He does grant prayers, sometimes in an instant, others it may take a while. But most of the time, he grants it by allowing you to realize what you have in order to see how to reach that goal. So if you pray for a miracle, a change may come, be ready – it's going to be a life-changing moment. It's going to be a revelation.

When prayer turns from 'Help' into "Thank You" I realized you become more giving. You realize how much you have and find all the more reasons to give back.

PITSTOP ⬤

*I can do all things through
Christ who strengthens me.*

—Philippians 4:13

I believe that God won't give you anything which you can't handle. Every time I'm faced with problems, I am reminded by that saying. The rationale for the reassurance is that no matter how hopeless a situation may be, just remember that God won't give us problems we can't handle, and if we remember that, we can make it through another day. I know things happen for a reason, yet sometimes it gets so overwhelming. As the saying goes, 'When it rains, it pours.' There are times, problems just come pouring in, one after the other. That's how I felt when my career wasn't going the way I wanted it to go. Then my favorite uncle died. My wife and I struggled to have a child for eight years. How can God, who is good, put me in situations which could break my heart and discourage me all at the same time? But because I believed God knows I can handle it, I believed I was strong so I was able to overcome it.

Looking back, I wasn't strong enough. You know what anchored me? Yes, God. He allowed all of these events to happen because He was preparing me for what's to come. God allowed things to happen to me – sometimes too much to bear – because He wants me to be ready for the future He has planned and that He will be with me all the way. I know that I cannot be without Him. I need to have faith that He will provide. God gives these challenges and difficulties in life and then shows you His care and responsiveness through the people around you. A friend, a family member, a colleague even your fellow church member. They are there in solidarity with you so you don't have to do it alone when everything is too much to bear. Saying a prayer to Him humbles me and reminds me that I cannot do all things on my own. We need God and you have the choice to turn Him away or embrace His grace and see Him as your Savior.

Wednesday Bible Study Group headed by Sam Liuson.

So how must we pray? I believe in praying with hope. Because why else would you be praying if you're not hoping for something to change. With faith comes hope and in prayer you find the strength to find it in you what you need to do.

People who successfully cultivate hope in their lives don't become paralyzed by seemingly insurmountable problems. They get involved. They do the good that they can, in the place where they are, with the tools and the people around them. They find concrete and local opportunities to engage the work of redeeming our world.[25]

For me my faith is what has helped me to overcome life's big hurdles. I think anyone who believes in God can say the same thing. They say pray until something happens. Prayer is power. It is more powerful than magic. Pray regularly and you can actually see the shift in your life. I know mine did and it has continually transformed my life and those I love.

Perhaps some of you may have your own religion or don't even believe in God. Although I am still a "work in progress", God has always been with me. He is my true north. ◄►

---

[25] Robert Hardies, "Three Ways to Cultivate A Sense of Hope, Even When Times Seem Hopeless," The Washington Post, December 21, 2016, https://www.washingtonpost.com/news/acts-of-faith (accessed March 2017)

JUMPSTART

- Daily prayer is a practice in focus and discipline which emotionally and spiritually prepares you each day.

- A strong faith creates a strong foundation and furthers a business.

- My faith contributes to the success of my business because it has helped me to see things clearly and see the opportunities along the way and find solutions to my problems.

- Ask = Pray. Seek = Pray more. Knock = Pray constantly and be persistent.

- God allows things you can't handle to happen to you NOT because you can handle them, but because He wants you to know that He is there for you and He will walk with you through the pain by giving us other people to help us through it.

- Pray with hope and believe that God will deliver His promise.

FINAL THOUGHTS

The Journey Continues

Thank you for joining me on this journey. I know that for some of you, it may not have been easy. Some of the lessons or ideas presented here challenge most, if not everything, that we believed in.

Death is what gives life meaning. Death poses a challenge to one's ability to live a meaningful life. If our lives will end and we will soon be forgotten, what is the point of everything that we do?

What would you do if this was your last day on earth?

In my case, a lot. So much so that it literally changed my life. The thought of death made Frances and I turn our lives around in ways we never thought we could, but we did. And this is what I shared in this book.

Memories made together last a lifetime.
Team Blade trip to Sunway Lagoon, Kuala Lumpur, Malaysia

This book began as an e-mail about my thoughts when I gave up something that I truly loved. Seven years later, I am living a whole new story –the best story of my life.

For too long, we have been told that change is hard. That change takes too long. It will need an amount of time to happen. In our case, it just took a compelling reason and a burning desire to shape our own destiny. It happened in an instant.

Mirage Club gathering, Philippine Arena, 2014

My intention, in writing this book, is to encourage you to gain the power to become your own storyteller.

We are all in different places in the journey. In the beginning, it will be a struggle. Negative thoughts would pop up and sometimes it may feel like you are trying to fool yourself into becoming something you are not. With practice, you can become skilled and you can spot which part of your life is working and which isn't.

First Edition

What Would You Do?

If This Was Your Last Day On Earth

7 Lessons Life Taught Me

You're NEVER Too Old To Start Over Again!

Robertson Sy Tan

Foreword by Francis Kong

Do negative thoughts still continue to pop up in my head? Yes. For as long I have lived, I notice that there are still thoughts that are holding me back. Any feeling, attitude, or thought that doesn't feel quite right is a negative piece. But by now, I can quickly correct it in my mind. This creates a shift in me. It creates a change which I can feel in an instant. And in this book, I have shown you how you can create that change for yourself.

God has plans for everyone. God loves us all. Have faith. He will show you the way. Whatever challenges life throws at you, keep in mind that you are just being prepared for a bigger purpose.

And now, finally you have this book in your hands in which I share the best stories and lessons of my life and my life's journey.

Make every day, every minute count, and start sharing your own stories. In the end, success cannot be measured by how much money or achievements you've made. The biggest measure of your success is the lives you've touched.

As Mahatma Gandhi famously said, "You must be the change you want to see in the world." So from here on, live your day as if there is no tomorrow. You will notice positive changes that will come your way. ❧

To invite Robert to speak in your school or university, email him at RST@ThatGuyInRed.com or send a message in Facebook or Instagram.
Keyword: That Guy In Red

www.ingramcontent.com/pod-product-compliance
Lightning Source LLC
Chambersburg PA
CBHW020203060426
42445CB00031B/188